CRYPTOGRAMS

PUZZLE BOOK FOR ADULTS

500 Large Print Cryptogram Puzzles To Improve Memory
And Sharpen Brain

Stephen J. Ellis

Table of Contents

How To Play

A cryptogram is a popular puzzle game which is widely used for entertainment purposes. The puzzles are **short quotes and phrases** which are **encrypted** using a simple substitution code.

In this book, there are 500 cryptogram puzzles. Each puzzle is a quote made by a famous personality. <u>Each quote is encrypted in such a way that each letter of the alphabet is a substitute for another letter.</u>

<u>For Example</u>:

PLZ UZTP MIQ PK JGZRYWP PLZ OAPAGZ YT PK WGZIPZ YP. - IUGILIN DYHWKDH

The above is a cryptogram puzzle for the below quote…

THE BEST WAY TO PREDICT THE FUTURE IS TO CREATE IT. - ABRAHAM LINCOLN

In this example, the letter 'P' represents the letter 'T', 'L' represents 'H', 'Z' represents 'E', and so on. Your **objective** is to figure out the code to solve each puzzle.

Tips

So, you finally got hold of the new set of cryptogram puzzles that your peers were talking about. And you cannot wait to simply start to solve them!

But wait, all of these puzzles look a bit unnerving. How do you even start? Well, like any other kind of puzzle, there are some tactics.

Here are 8 tips for the beginner who is unsure of how to solve cryptogram puzzles.

1. One-Letter Words:

Always begin with the one-letter words in your cryptogram. After all, there are only a few letters that can be used as a word. The most common of these letters are **'a' and 'I'**. When you have these letters figured out, go on replacing the cipher (the substitute letter) throughout the cryptogram.

2. Most Commonly Used Letters:

In an English sentence, some letters repeat more frequently than others. So, to solve your cryptogram, look for the ciphers that occur at a higher frequency. More often than not, you should be able to decode these ciphers as one of the 6 letters, **E, T, A, O, I, and N**. And if you've already decoded 'I' and 'A' as in tip #1, this step moves forward quickly.

3. Double Letters:

Very few words have double letters in them, such as 'OO', or 'EE', or 'LL'. Examples include 'Door', 'Feel', 'Well', etc. So, look for the words that have double letters and try to decode the cipher. The easiest way to do this is to get your spelling brain activated and focusing on the letters that come before and after the double letters.

4. Contractions:

Contractions are a way to join two words with an apostrophe. They are used majorly in dialogues or extremely informal writing. Examples include **don't, won't, you're, she's, it's,** and so on . Spot these apostrophes and try to understand the letter appearing right next to each apostrophe. If you have possessive contractions, such as "man's", "cat's", or "tree's", it becomes easier to decipher the letter 's'.

5. Digraphs:

Some letters appear commonly in pairs. The best example is 'Th' in words such as 'Them', or 'They', or 'This'. The easiest would be to figure out a 'The' if you've already found out the cipher for the letter "e".

6. Two and Three-Letter Words:

These are the next words you should tackle in your cryptogram. Popular two-letter words include 'am', 'an', 'is', 'it', 'of', 'to', 'go', and so on. Three-letter words are a little tougher but if you can crack down common ones such as 'are', 'the', 'and', etc., solving the puzzle becomes a lot easier.

7. Unused Letters:

This trick comes in handy when you're almost done with the puzzle, yet cannot get the last bits straightened out. Take a good look at your semi-solved puzzle and think of the letters in the English alphabet that have not been used. Do any of them drill any sense into your unsolved sections? More often than not, they do!

8. Use a Pencil:

Guessing and making mistakes is a part of solving cryptograms. Use a pencil so you can correct your guesses if they're wrong.

Logic:

Lastly, you must apply your logic to solve the puzzle. And that's because, well, it's a puzzle and it's an exercise for your brain. You need to keep a cool head and apply pure logic to decode what's in front of you. And if you're playing at a contest and need to keep score, your cool head will matter much more than any of the above tricks.

So now, back to your puzzle and have a great time decoding the "secret message".

If Needed, A HINT For Each Puzzle Is Offered Starting On Page 171. If You Get Stuck On A Puzzle, The Complete SOLUTIONS For All Puzzles Start On Page 185.

PUZZLES

1.

ZON UTHZ BTUUTS AKE GNTGIN DRJN XG

ZONRQ GTANQ RH WE ZORSLRSD ZONE

MTS'Z OKJN KSE. - KIRBN AKILNQ

. . . .

2.

HBD QDKADH VN QJKKDQQ EQ HV GV HBD

KVYYVU HBEUW JUKVYYVUFX ODFF. - TVBU

G. AVKZDNDFFDA TA

. . . .

3.

YXL NTQY PUQYLJ TA JUSQ HQ TRL

PHYXTIY OUIEXYLK. - L. L. FINNHREQ

. . . .

4.

Q GLO'K GILONY KIY ZQMYGKQSO SV KIY CQOZ, EBK Q GLO LZDBFK TU FLQPF KS LPCLUF MYLGI TU ZYFKQOLKQSO. - DQTTU ZYLO

. . . .

5.

VOVXP DKFV ZEFVDCKYR UEUZ KY FP CVSA, K DCKYG DNKLV STEQD KD SYA K AE KD SYPNSP. - RKWTVXD REDDJXKVA

. . . .

6.

VBKL IFS'TK XFU ZFWKUBYLX UF HGFTK, UBKGK'Z LFUBYLX XGKPUKG UBPL P ABPMMKLXK. - UKGGI NGPQZBPV

. . . .

7.

TDLZ Q WLV IC CO TDYV Q YN, Q ALMCNL

TDYV Q NQIDV AL. - WYC VXH

. . . .

8.

QW AXBC ASLCG JUMCLUN MUO SB PRBC

CU NXFZX CGX NSHGCB UM. - PUFM LSZXLB

. . . .

9.

CP CM BKOCFA EKO BIOHLMP XEXLFPM

PWIP SL XKMP YEDKM PE MLL PWL GCAWP.

- IOCMPEPGL EFIMMCM

. . . .

10.

BCPF TSK EPLMC ICP PFH SZ TSKE ESWP,

IJP L OFSI JF JI LFH CLFY SF. - ZELFOGJF H.

ESSVPAPGI

....

11.

KUPLFYJDW   JZ   YEK   GDZY   TDSKXIPA

SKFTDW SEJLE ODP LFW PZK YD LEFWCK

YEK SDXAU. - WKAZDW GFWUKAF

....

12.

UQBJ   QH   RKBHVDBV   GIKKP   VODV   AKW

NKEJH XH DBW NKEJH VK HJJ XH ODGGT. -

LJBMDCQB PIDBYNQB

....

13.

YQ OR UASR QT MKYYKCW YMR YJSWRY,

UMQQY TKSUY, JCN PJBB IMJYRLRS ZQA

MKY   YMR   YJSWRY.   -   JUMBRKWM

OSKBBKJCY

. . . .

14.

MOFT   EQSSQBYTWQOZ   BFD   GO

UPOMBUKO.   QW   QZ   UDTC   WJO

QKFHQDFMC   UDOZ   WJFW   FMO

YDBUDXYOMFGTO. - WJOUEUMO D. PFQT

. . . .

15.

USCAA   PRSOHSJ.   JR   IRY   AYRU,   JR   IRY

XFIECS FI MRLS ZRLSICM, KLY AYSFDC PRS

YBC GHSN ACY KCPRSC MRL. - ECRSEC

OBFYCPFCXJ

. . . .

16.

ZDOCP   UOY   ZDREYDZQ   UEZ   GBMOQD

QSVMM LMBVQEGBQ. - AVIPQRC UGRXC AG

. . . .

17.

JO NJD RA YGHLYO HD JRA DNG QBYAO
QBGGDH QDWWBGF HJO LOAIOQH DU
DHJOLA. - BETOLH ORGAHORG

. . . .

18.

SH'R QBH LKTH DBM PBBY TH HKTH
ATHHZGR, SH'R LKTH DBM RZZ. - KZQGD
JTFSJ HKBGZTM

. . . .

19.

SE MFJ BKY OSASUN FJI FE B PYUPY FE
FCOSNBISFU MFJ BKY B POBAY. - XK.
DBMUY XMYK

. . . .

20.

SNE FWS YWGK XN TDMYX W QWXXHK FNJK XYWZ NZBK XN LDZ DX. - FWJMWJKX XYWXBYKJ

. . . .

21.

QJJF DJM LGT LGOKI XJS KJLOYT VSL KJ JKT TQRT KJLOYTR. - MOYF MSVOK

. . . .

22.

LINGGCDJCV NPC HINS KNAC GERC EDSCPCVSEDJ. YUCPLYKEDJ SICK EV HINS KNACV GERC KCNDEDJRXG. - FYVIXN KNPEDC

. . . .

23.

SZYT AMTV XMR MDT BMF EXBRJZXO

NTLEFVT SZYT JEV ESITEAB OZWTX BMF

TWTIBRJZXO. - IESKJ QEIVRMX

. . . .

24.

QASX SFSCJYATXB TN OWHTXB JWIC QPJ,

JWI'CS TX YAS QCWXB GPXS. - NYSFSX

QCTBAY

. . . .

25.

XIOOIM OA WNKUO Q HQZBWI OUQZ OA

HJMLI OUI BQMGZILL. - HUNZILI VMARIMX

. . . .

26.

YD ST ITSLDJ IBGD IBND. YD XTSWHCD BE.

- GBXVB JTPBS

27.

BFPRFXDSJT SM TJD HDDHSTHOYF, OWD
SR ZF XQHMF BFPRFXDSJT ZF XHT XHDXQ
FUXFYYFTXF. - KSTXF YJIOHPVS

28.

DXMU JDZ RQJ JDZ'PU EDNXE GD RUGGCU
KDP RUMDXV, GAQG'R YAQG AQHHUXR GD
JDZ NX CNKU. - TDAX K. FUXXUVJ

29.

PX PZEEZHW ZW GZDM ZE WHN PMSMGX
NH EOSKZKM, ION NH NFSZKM. - PCXC
CWTMGHO

30.

YQUUFYY QYQNTTM UGDFY BG BAGYF CAG

NEF BGG KQYM BG KF TGGSWRV ZGE WB. -

AFREM XNIWX BAGEFNQ

. . . .

31.

WX   BCJLWSYU   OJ   BPLUX   W   JLUFFOXV

JLBXU. - FAUJSBLL

. . . .

32.

NDUKDOD VSPV UKAD KZ YGWVS UKOKXQ

PXT JGHW NDUKDA YKUU SDUB FWDPVD

VSD APFV. - YKUUKPI LPIDZ

. . . .

33.

BS NYS BRNL BS YSISNLSEZT EM. SJXSZZSKXS, LRSK, GV KML NK NXL, UWL N RNUGL. - NYGVLMLZS

. . . .

34.

TOTWUNJMLD JFI QTFENU, QEN LGN TOTWUGLT ITTI MN. - PGLKEPMEI

. . . .

35.

UQZTPQO YILLC, P WQHLICYFQH YVL NLFQPQO ZB RFYPLQKL. UQZTPQO OIFCC, P KFQ FRRILKPFYL RLICPCYLQKL. - VFJ GZIJFQH

. . . .

36.

FL QS GFLC FO UPFEU NP QCVE VESNDFEU,

F DVYC NP GFYC FN QSOCGL. - HFAT
HFPHIVE

. . . .

37.

VCUVGC REC QUEC TQVECFFCB JA PKC

VULCE UZ USE CDRQVGC ERPKCE PKRI PKC

CDRQVGC UZ USE VULCE. - JTGG YGTIPUI

. . . .

38.

GAXOAXK JTAX ZMGQ HMOS DXKVO

OSTADSOP. OT EKBMKLK MG OSK SKXTMW

ZVRKP SKXTKP. - EKGUVZMG QMPXVKBM

. . . .

39.

XZNW ZA CFD LTFOD YFM NLAD KFO POC FP
YFM YZUY KFO EXZJT, TOD YFM MWXX KFO
TFOCEW. - RZRZLC SFJFPZ

. . . .

40.

CUELXA OPU UP GA H CDYYACC, GDU
EHUJAE UP GA PI XHFDA. - HFGAEU
ALOCUALO

. . . .

41.

YH YZ IXHHXB HG DOSX O WXOTYTLKRC
CYKX OTA WOMX O AYKKXBXTUX HDOT HG
WXBXCN DOSX O CGTL CYKX. - IBNOTH D.
WULYCC

. . . .

23

42.

X FZ GOYA JDZFO, FYSJGDPJ X VCPVCS XS.

- ZFVM SEFXO

. . . .

43.

FMAUA SW JKTE JKA LJFSZGFSJK, GKY FMGF SW YAWSUA. KJ UAGWJKW JU BUSKQSBTA QJKFGSK SF JU WFGKY GIGSKWF SF. - NGKA WLSTAE

. . . .

44.

NRBYB HX PQNRHPI XQ GXBCBXX ZX KQHPI BWWHMHBPNCF NRZN ERHMR XRQGCK PQN OB KQPB ZN ZCC. - ABNBY KYGMJBY

. . . .

45.

YKHPYIPA SP FGB QGFP GBE FIGCCPBHPV
GV LPPR GV YIP KFPGB GBL GV IZHI GV YIP
VDE. - VKBZG HGBLIZ

. . . .

46.

WRN'EF   JRXXO   YOMSF   GKUF   XCFZF'B
MRHRYW   QOXSCKMJ.   -   QKGGKOI   Q.
ANZUFW

. . . .

47.

CSCVALKOXJ APD NHX OQHJOXC OM VCHT.
- IHRTP IONHMMP

. . . .

48.

ADRF YFDYCF CDDE UDT J NFJWQVUWC
YCJKF. DQBFTA RJEF J YCJKF
NFJWQVUWC. - BJITJQ VZJMJQ EBJZ

. . . .

49.

MLYYLG YW RW KWFLYIHSU HFCLGBLNYPQ
YIDS YW RW SWYIHSU BPDZPLKKPQ. -
GWMLGY KNIJPPLG

. . . .

50.

WPT ATHW WPCJIH CJ ZCGT EVT GVTT. WPT
HTNYJB ATHW WPCJIH EVT MTVO
TKFTJHCMT. - NYNY NPEJTZ

. . . .

51.

TOKKITT RT WVA SRWNM, SNRMOYI RT WVA

SNANM. RA RT ALI KVOYNPI AV KVWARWOI

ALNA KVOWAT. - DRWTAVW KLOYKLRMM

. . . .

52.

F XWOM EK CRMJFWV BWVMEB. F WL KEVS

RWCCFKEWBMVS   JYGFKYC.   -   WVQMGB

MFECBMFE

. . . .

53.

ZDYYFOSXX QRVSO XOSDTX FO VZCQLUZ D

MQQC GQL MFMO'V TOQK GQL JSRV QYSO.

- EQZO IDCCGWQCS

. . . .

54.

SQWVX UF MBV VXQ NYQWVQFV ZBFF UM
ZUJQ. VXQ NYQWVQFV ZBFF UF HXWV
SUQF UMFUSQ DF HXUZQ HQ ZUKQ. -
MBYRWM GBDFUMF

. . . .

55.

K DETP QPEIJPH RTPI XDP CPEIO XDEX
NDPJ RJP'O ZKJH KO ZEHP FV, XDKO
HKZKJKODPO BPEI. - IROE VEILO

. . . .

56.

ZH JAW NADBZDWM BA BOZDX BOM VFJ
JAW'QM FSVFJL BOAWROB, JAW'SS
NADBZDWM BA RMB VOFB JAW'QM FSVFJL
RAB. - XMQZD BKWGMFW

57.

NQCK NC PZBLRC ZU GCDUAC GCZZCB

ZQSK NC SBC, CRCBIZQLKX SBUHKE HP

GCDUACP GCZZCB ZUU. - VSHYU DUCYQU

58.

QX   QA   LWXXWN   XJ   RHQC   QD

JNQVQDHCQXB XUHD XJ AIKKWWP QD

QGQXHXQJD. - UWNGHD GWCEQCCW

59.

MSF HR TJWS IHY AHFHYS GIQ, JGV MSF HR

TJWS IHY VYSJTR FITIYYIQ'R YSJMDFZ. -

TJMJMJ ZIHRJANJD

60.

LZS YTAAFSUU DY ABYS BU DFAP
IOOSUUBMAS BF LZS VESUSFL JDJSFL. -
SOQZIEL LDAAS

. . . .

61.

LZ IDH NORU UD TLYQ O BOFFI TLZQ, ULQ
LU UD O VDOT, RDU UD FQDFTQ DX
UBLRVC. - OTMQXU QLRCUQLR

. . . .

62.

LXRHXIFJL QR WPH POIR HP IXYPUXI, TOH
HPVPIIPA QR POIR HP AQW PI MPRX. -
MLWFPW KPNWRPW

. . . .

63.

T EVQEAJ QEMNKW NB IK JBZKIBWA, IXN

MBQ T DKEVTCK T JLBXVW LEPK IKKM ZBDK

JFKOTSTO. - VTVA NBZVTM

. . . .

64.

CU KGHHUZ OSZU SHAUP BP BOJRBPJABSP

AYJP BP ZUJXBAN. - KUPUWJ

. . . .

65.

TE TJ BWJTBK EC LNTRO JEKCHP

GATROKBH EAWH EC KBVWTK LKCQBH

DBH. - ZKBOBKTGQ OCNPRWJJ

. . . .

66.

NLW'J FQU BUQJUANGB'Q QJGJU LE OVWN,
JL OGXU JLNGB'Q NURVQVLW. - R.
WSVWKCG QOVJC

. . . .

67.

URTV RW OVP IVQHVPO DZMO ZMIIVPW OJ
LJF MPC PRPVOL IVQHVPO ZJD LJF
QVWIJPC OJ RO. - UJF ZJUOA

. . . .

68.

LBA CPZ BGNL CX IPZZ CX LBA MDSGJ LBA
CPZ CGE IPZZEBV TSNN CNTCLX WZ CX
PZCN CX LBA WZNSZQZ SM MB WZ. -
PBWZPM V. EPCJZ

. . . .

69.

FDD GSL TRA RFXS FURYSXSH ZCSFB
BRYLZO RFXS MSSL ZCSFB HCSFGSCO. -
ACYOAL OTSBB GFCHSL

. . . .

70.

P BSTV GR CPUV VZVLRCWVLV, KFB DWV
TVVHD UPMQPMI WVL CSR KSAT. - WVMMR
REFMIGSM

. . . .

71.

TITBRYFXHU YFKY XBBXYKYTL JL KCMJY
MYFTBL WKH VTKA JL YM KH
JHATBLYKHAXHU ME MJBLTVITL. - WKBV
ZJHU

. . . .

72.

KQLRH XQL UJFH KL IJAB SARHFJGBZ PJW JPQAHNH TFHJKBZ. - OLQW I. VHWWHUZ

. . . .

73.

QSY RYFCUFPU VFCY PMQSTW HQU LF QV VCNTSYF   LSU   QV   PSEEFFWNHR   CU UMNHRP NH TNVF UMCU WQH'U YFCTTB JCUUFY. - VYCHENP EMCH

. . . .

74.

XC KRC ORWTQC KRWK GSE LBUR KS UCC BT KRC LSNYF. - ZWRWKZW QWTFRB

. . . .

75.

LND QEL XHCI SMA VNUBS ACAQL NU GABS

XUHACI HC LNDUBATX. - ACWTHBM

YUNOAUG

. . . .

76.

FO XLO OPHIPOK QH ZOXLSU DHL

COXVMVN WAQ AIQMCXQOIG IMDO UXZ

VHVO. - VXPXI LXPMTXVQ

. . . .

77.

DQW FTWOCRETWG BENW EK TUD SUPDQ

BEYETV. - KUAPCDWK

. . . .

78.

CNA'L OM SWRYMC OP PNWZ SZNOUMDR, OM UMC OP PNWZ CZMQDR. - ZQUSY EQUCN MDMZRNA

. . . .

79.

JWUJ'F NQI FVUOO FJIK PND U VUQ, NQI MZUQJ OIUK PND VUQXZQY. - QIZO UDVFJDNQM

. . . .

80.

GHBBRQTDD RD GHWRQX H MHVXT, MNWRQX, IHVRQX, IMNDT AQRO PHZRMK RQ HQNOGTV IROK. - XTNVXT SYVQD

. . . .

81.

XM OFT ETCJK AKFARK, OFT GINK ZF YXWK
YF RFNK YGKW. - WFYGKV YKVKBI

. . . .

82.

BMR TAEW BA IDOORII PI EKSEZI DJWRT
OAJIBTDOBPAJ. - KPKZ BALKPJ

. . . .

83.

BQ LW EUUR BSWBX HFGU GSW FWDG
MWFGZAN, EWBXWAQ LHEE JW GSUQW
LSU WICULWA UGSWAQ. - JHEE OBGWQ

. . . .

84.

TOY AM TD AMMRY VG JADB VZYF JTQQYF.
AG WVR BVD'Q JADB, AQ BVYMD'Q JTQQYF.
- JTFS QXTAD

85. SCFYE TNEECA TCFBONGE NPCLA FYE

NEWFCKY LEAGO ARYW VANKA DYAAGED

PYAAYK ANVAY GE ARYF. - PGOO FNRYK

86.

PB PRS'B BLA QINSBCPSR CLACW BI VJPQD

BLCB OACZ UIN INB, PB'R BLA TADDJA PS

UINZ RLIA. - QNLCQQCW CJP

87.

FNA UOI KXVV O LENIXXM WF KJX OMMNHD

EI JED WOUY. - WXCXMVF MAWEY

88.

KWJV WP KWFV U ETI TJ MQTMTKUGVP.
STO BVHVA FBTN NQUG STO'AV CTWBC GT
CVG. - JTAAVPG COZD

. . . .

89.

MJH WBXZZHWM XEM DO TPYSYHWW PW
VDCMJ BDCH MJXY MJH RCHXMHWM
PYMHYMPDY. - TXJZPZ RPGCXY

. . . .

90.

LP ZRQVV OWQNT L IKP TCG CA
VHVQUZRLPY L'HV SVKQPVN KJWCZ SLDV.
LZ YWVT WP. - QWJVQZ DQWTZ

. . . .

91.

UPJUM CF TWTP UY VT GYJQS CQ
FCZIOCECUH, LQS QYU CQ UMT
ZJOUCIOCECUH LQS EYQGJFCYQ YG
UMCQXF. - CFLLE QTRUYQ

. . . .

92.

WCC KRWK VI WMI AJ KRI MIJLCK PY VRWK
VI RWHI KRPLZRK. - FLEERW

. . . .

93.

I HSXXWVWXM WX I HSOXJZ PGJ GIX GIL MJ
KWXMSZ MJ MJJ VIZF JHMWVWXMX. - LJZ
VIOURWX

. . . .

94.

XGMJ AH Y NARANPEN CV HQPYU. UKP
OCTP SCG HQPYU, UKP XGMJAPT SCG DPU.
- TYS JTCM

. . . .

95.

PO SJQ DAPXR SJQ MYZ DJJ FKMII DJ KMRZ
M TPOOZYZXEZ, DYS FIZZWPXL NPDA M
KJFHQPDJ. - TMIMP IMKM

. . . .

96.

MCBJBAPDBNG BL NWT XBAT PCN MX
CTITIVTCBAJ YWPN GMO WTPC VON
XMCJTNNBAJ YWTCT GMO WTPCR BN. -
DPOCTAUT Z. ETNTC

. . . .

97.

NOX STYL YQFQN NS SCA AXHYQEHNQST SB NSFSAASG GQYY JX SCA KSCJNU SB NSKHL. - BAHTDYQT K. ASSUXMXYN

. . . .

98.

UWQEYBQEWT EL MDBQ VNQL OWH LQBJQNC. DBKEQ EL MDBQ PNNAL OWH VWETV. - XEU JWDT

. . . .

99.

H FJUEIHPY OUAYI OGRR PUF RDHXD IU YDDM HP GVMADIIGUP HI UPD YDDY. - JDPAGS GZIDP

. . . .

100.

UGEU OGVPG JAZI XAU YVFF CI KEYZI CI

IUQAXDZQ. - BQVZJQVPG XVZURIPGZ

. . . .

101.

MY OSW'QT LSMDL HUQSWLU UTCC, ZTTB

LSMDL. - JMDXHSD NUWQNUMCC

. . . .

102.

PLTTALQJ AB YRJ XHZE NLT AH NRAUR EXD

BZJJW NAYR YRJ JHJPE. - CTLHUXAB FJ ZL

TXURJCXDULDZF

. . . .

103.

CZPA WQK ZLDP L ONPLE, WQK'DP RQU UQ

RNLS TU LAO APDPN JPU RQ. - HLNQJ

SKNAPUU

. . . .

104.

OULUN HS KS I GSFKSN JWSXU SZZRFU

ABIOKX WILU GRUG. - UNYI QSYQUFT

. . . .

105.

UWUS FL HTZ'QU TS BIU QFVIB BQNPE,

HTZ'JJ VUB QZS TWUQ FL HTZ KZYB YFB

BIUQU. - RFJJ QTVUQY

. . . .

106.

BMSZ EDX JDGVNZR GBMG MCC GBZ

QZDQCZ VJ PMSDK DP YVKGB NDJGKDC

MKZ MCKZMRE YDKJ? - YZJJE BVCC

. . . .

107.

IMIF HG H YFIJ PWZP PRQRAARJ PWI JRABT JRNBT LR PR CHIUIE, H JRNBT EPHBB CBZFP QS ZCCBI PAII. - QZAPHF BNPWIA

. . . .

108.

MBY AIHD TYEJAI DAO REY SYJMLIYS MA KYZAWY LJ MBY TYEJAI DAO SYZLSY MA KY. - ERHTB CRHSA YWYEJAI

. . . .

109.

GSALKQ CEWL LWLAURPLAL UEF DE. CLX ME EML LWLA ZEVL XE UEF RBXPEFX CLKWBMD PKSSBLA. - VEXPLA XLALGK

. . . .

110.

RVQX JDZDYID VLIYZD, PQCX KTD MYGD

AJPWYK WJPR YK. - TVJADJ CDD

. . . .

111.

FCG'D KR JXZJPF DC IPQR MS DLR ICCF DC

IC XCZ DLR IZRJD. - WCLG F. ZCTERXRVVRZ

. . . .

112.

ZLJZLDHPE   BZDACATC   AT   P   GBJVL

CHEDAZEALJ. - VBEAQ ZBSLEE

. . . .

113.

ARO WGWOV TXYIJW VRI EOW EYNOV VRI

PRUW 60 UWBRYHU RA QELLXYWUU. -

OEPLQ DEPHR WTWOURY

. . . .

114.

Z'I VZTC GQ QGSSGBZEW IR UONHIV. Z'I
FKVP WGZEW PG HVC BANON PANR'ON
WGZEW HEU AGGC KY BZPA PANI SHPNO. -
IZPTA ANUJNOW

. . . .

115.

AFNYBOXN BHX SBHY GI YLX REXN YLBY
GVX SBCN IGH B IEZZ ZFIX. - NGSLFB ZGHXV

. . . .

116.

RYYN OZFMRJ XYLP OY APYAIP HZY HWFO,
QDO QPOOPU OZFMRJ XYLP OY OZYJP HZY
RY YDO WMN RPO OZPL. - WMYMGLYDJ

. . . .

117.

Y KL CQKEBGAJ GWM KJJ WG CQWIN PQW
IKYU EW CW LN. YC'I HNVKAIN WG CQNL Y'L
UWYEF YC LXINJG. - KJHNMC NYEICNYE

. . . .

118.

RIXO   SFAMYO, RIXO JZZVNRS. - RIBCB
QZGR

. . . .

119.

KPS'R FVVE Z JZS LNVYYTSL RPP IPSL. AV'Y
YNBV RP MTSK RAV ZSYHVB YPJVHAVBV
VIYV. - JZV HVYR

. . . .

120.

WGFCAWL AN AOKGNNATZS. FCS IGBX
AFNSZQ NMUN A'O KGNNATZS. - MHXBSU
CSKTHBW

. . . .

121.

JBB UMT SWWA QI BMZW. PTG J BQGGBW
LYMLMBJGW SMR JSA GYWS AMWIS'G
YTDG. - LYJDBWI ILYTBV

. . . .

122.

BUA HU KUL TCKH LIQ IRSSB JCTQ. BUA
ORWQ CL. - XROCJJR QBFCKY WCOPRJJ

. . . .

123.

BXA'Q PIS JRPZTMR WQ'M XERI, MCWNR JRPZTMR WQ DZKKRARB. - NTBVWH LZPXJXVMUW

. . . .

124.

T GIDK KW FS YTBS GIKSU. T GIDK KW HYTX KLUWNJL QTDJSUH, FNK LWYV NX I HLTX. - ZTALSYYS GTYYTIZH

. . . .

125.

CKIQJA QA SIK NKUDKIG QIANQUZGQSI, IQIKGE-IQIK NKUDKIG NKUANQUZGQSI. - GOSTZA Z. KPQASI

. . . .

126.

XIDHD QHD JDXXDH RXQHXDHR XIQK FD,
JLX V'F Q RXHCKS GVKVRIDH. - LRQVK
JCMX

. . . .

127.

CVB XNIB ZNA CY MYWGQB AYWH TYKBA LX
CY IYQM LC YJBH YKFB NKM SWC LC LK
AYWH SYFEBC. - ELK VWGGNHM

. . . .

128.

HVD BDCK FVK SGK UFHVFG RGZQFG HVDE
SQBQKC OGAUDCG VZ YNGEG HVD AVBG
ZEVB. HVDE VFSH SQBQK QC HVDE CVDS. -
YUSK RQCFGH

. . . .

129.

LC CT LC PCU. UODTD ZB PC UTW. - WCLH

. . . .

130.

RNS MSAQSR YT V NVHHC IVQQGVXS

QSIVGJM V MSAQSR. - NSJJC CYWJXIVJ

. . . .

131.

XWRP JPA FOIE GPZONRP FDPM DOSP

RTJPFDWAL FT ROM. KTTIR, GPZONRP

FDPM DOSP FT ROM RTJPFDWAL. - YIOFT

. . . .

132.

BOH IUBO BL WGPPHWW FW BL BUYH

JUWWFCH, VHBHTJFSHV UPBFLS. - BLSZ

TLKKFSW

52

. . . .

133.

QVWCF ENVK NGJ FKOYIA, NK ANIONJO

OCAO GWCC RWKO ENV XN QVWCF

XROWKA. - HYKKYR ZKYE

. . . .

134.

FRWV   SCZ   LZFG   NV   QZTVIEXLLT

NCSBKCITE   NQX   RX   HQEX   NV   FRMVT

WLIKCITE. - ELIVZ BRVIBVJCCIT

. . . .

135.

DWNG WT NBKS OYG WRTWZG KFO. VYGR

JKF   TYWNO   KR   OYG   WRTWZG,   DWNG

TYWNOT   KR   OYG   KFOTWZG.   -   QCSCD

BCAWQCRO

. . . .

136.

LXO XIEYOE LXO AILLRO, LXO NTOOLOE
LXO MBFLWEJ. - RON AEWTD

. . . .

137.

PLZ UZTP MIQ PK JGZRYWP PLZ OAPAGZ YT
PK WGZIPZ YP. - IUGILIN DYHWKDH

. . . .

138.

YP JWD QIBH HBHXJSQYVR DVOHX
TWVSXWM, JWD'XH VWS ZWBYVR PIAS
HVWDRQ. - ZIXYW IVOXHSSY

. . . .

139.

IRNX QOFG XOF WBXFSLHJJBS XOCRZOX
XOF QCSJA QBN FGAHGZ, OF XRSGFA
HGXC B VRXXFSEJD. - LSCTFSV

. . . .

140.

KO PGD SINFKUIH EGZ VGZISODF PGDS
QEGDYEQR NSI, PGD ZGDFH MIBIS QEKMC
N MIYNQKBI QEGDYEQ. - VINTI VKFYSKX

. . . .

141.

PU RWT NUU AOZVKLO VAOUZN VTJB POUT
PU RWT NUU AOZVKLO VKZNUJXUN. -
CZKRU JUU

. . . .

142.

N VUMQ FO BINPJWZM QE IUTZ UPP QIZ QINMYH N BERPJM'Q UXXEWJ. QIZM N VUMQ QE FETZ NM VNQI QIZF. - SIOPPNH JNPPZW

. . . .

143.

YAGYEP KYHO Y IZIYA OSSZVI, OXOB GDOB IDO ZLLP YVO YRYQBPI EZF. - YVBZAL TYAKOV

. . . .

144.

SGZ KTTH ANRZ NV NEVCNPZH YL ATWZ IEH KMNHZH YL DETUAZHKZ. - YZPSPIEH PMVVZAA

. . . .

145.

YAZH AI JSQ BHGICLHE OK QWH JCBOHL SZ
OLHGQWI RH QGVH, OCQ OK QWH BSBHJQI
QWGQ QGVH SCL OLHGQW GRGK. - BGKG
GJTHYSC

. . . .

146.

DLFZF OZF DJX AZFOD QOHY PG O
NFZYXG'Y BPKF. DLF QOH JF OZF IXZG OGQ
DLF QOH JF QPYUXCFZ JLH. - JPBBPOR
IOZUBOH

. . . .

147.

WSFYJ RFWW EOYU TGD JUGL, OYIF HGXF
EOYU TGD WOGL. - LQRRQYH
WOYJFWSFYXF

. . . .

148.

NERF LMHRF FEZPL NJBSC WJB RFFHYQF ZA WJB XPHN WJB TJBSC PJF ARZS? - MJVHMF E. DTEBSSHM

. . . .

149.

DYAHSQL JYMA LGLCSLP, WMK GLQLA DYAHLK KNLSA GTCLP. - FYNG D. ELGLGBJ

. . . .

150.

SXZU XK LUXHR IH DBU EXYU, UAUYPDBXHR USKU XK NWKD EMXDXHR. - FMYS EMSSUHOM

. . . .

151.

RX'F PHX VHJ LQGV SHQ VDNI XVDX LDCIF
AIHAZI ZHHC QA XH SHQ, RX'F JVH SHQ DYI.

- IZNRF AYIFZIS

. . . .

152.

MTRMVW   KEJJER   XEFUV   QJEX   M
BUWWGXGWD. YU REF'D UNBUID GD KMIZ.

- EWIMJ RGTOU

. . . .

153.

A EPZF RJPNF OJP ILK NYAEF AK RSPQDEF.

- EFPKLSCP CL ZAKIA

. . . .

154.

Y JICZ EZCZK YE NW PYUZ PZIKEZG IEWQJYET UKFN IEW NIE LJF ITKZZG LYQJ NZ. - GOGPZW UYZPG NIPFEZ

. . . .

155.

DFB IWYY AFS OQ LBAWNKQT JFE DFBE VAUQE, DFB IWYY OQ LBAWNKQT OD DFBE VAUQE. - OBTTKV

. . . .

156.

N FBTEO PFEETA PKFELO AKO GTDBS, IJA N PFE PFXA F XATEO FPDTXX AKO GFAOD AT PDOFAO QFEM DNRRBOX. - QTAKOD AODOXF

. . . .

157.

OSMPV NSM WVIHUEV OSVUW AMHHR IWV
QMO OWJV AMMHP. - ESJIQZEU

. . . .

158.

YBH SGKKHZHVTH LHYNHHV E DYACLXGVP
LXWTO EVS E DYHJJGVP DYWVH GD BWN
BGPB FWA ZEGDH FWAZ KWWY. - LHVVF
XHNGD

. . . .

159.

R IRMA CGLC CGP GLQAPQ R KYQT, CGP
SYQP NWHT R ZPPS CY GLOP. - CGYSLZ
FPIIPQZYM

. . . .

160.

YXH ASHIYPBO PIO'Y MXB PI CBPOC YB RHY JH. PY'I MXB PI CBPOC YB IYBD JH. - FUO TFON

. . . .

161.

JFG'R DLJCW WHUN JHB ZB RNW NHPEWIR BFL PWHM ZLR ZB RNW IWWJI RNHR BFL MXHGR. - PFZWPR XFLOI IRWEWGIFG

. . . .

162.

KYQKNY   EPQ   JPOFD   JPYB   DFQE YSYLBJPOFM ULY U MLYUJ UFFQBUFIY JQ JPQZY QW RZ EPQ GQ. - OZUUI UZOXQS

. . . .

163.

MTQX SLBXG CF PXLFTFW EIXF KCD YXOCPX PCSTRLSXH, GXS WCLMG LFH OILUWX LQSXU SIXP TF LF DFGSCAALYMX PLFFXU. - MXG YUCEF

. . . .

164.

AWG'B XKELVT DWL BTK SKEGJGY WD RJDK. XJSZRO HK ZLKXKGB DWL BTK ZKWZRK OWP RWIK. - SEQJSK REYEVK

. . . .

165.

VDL VYET RX GIT VUMG DM JUMT. UG UX RH GD RX GD VUET DRCXTJETX GIT VUMG DM JUEUOV BTJJ. - EDJGYUCT

. . . .

166.

M'IR VUMARF YIRE UGF YIRE UGF YIRE
UQUMG MG HW AMVR UGF OXUO MC PXW M
CNSSRRF. - HMSXURA LYEFUG

. . . .

167.

UGM'H QVH HPV ZVFD GZ QGRAMT XV
TDVFHVD HPFM HPV VBKAHVJVMH GZ
YAMMAMT. - DGXVDH EAWGRFEA

. . . .

168.

AXAML HJVDEQA CWBC IA QCMHXA CS
QCMBKUEA NMSSTQ HK CWA JHKT BKT
VSHQSKQ DQ. - SQPBM IHETA

. . . .

169.

BZ'M JPZZPF ZU JP G WBUL YUF G CGD

ZTGL G MTPPN GWW DUKF WBYP. -

PWBHGJPZT QPLLD

. . . .

170.

MTP LBN SIR PBBK. TL UBC PTAA, UBC PMU

ITS M ASMN. - J. XWRPRKS ASBKR

. . . .

171.

CKOKP EKN NJK WKIP VW MNPQYQCD VZN

YKKH SVZ WPVT HEISQCD NJK DITK. - RIRK

PZNJ

. . . .

172.

LXM UGRF GV MQMBDLXGRZ. AXPL DHY

LXGRJ DHY NMSHUM. - NYFFXP

173.

UYM EHREBERAIP XYG CIKC EU EC HGU FGCCEVPM CYGAPR SMU GAU GT UYM XIK GT UYGCM RGEHS EU. - UQEJEI JAHHEHSYIL

174.

DT DJGPUPJQG QW WPZNPTN EPO VPT'Y JQSN BUP VXQTSW DW ZOGU DW EPO VP. - VEJDT YUPZDW

175.

RHRPKILYOB KVN'HR RHRP CZOIRX YD VO ILR VILRP DYXR VU URZP. - BRVPBR ZXXZYP

176.

EGMK GA 10 WKPVKOQ IBCQ BCWWKOA QS
HA COT 90 WKPVKOQ BSI IK PKCVQ QS GQ.

- TKOOGA W. RGZYPS

. . . .

177.

BIN TFRB WUKKUVEHB BIUZO UR BIN
WNVURUFZ BF GVB, BIN SNRB UR TNSNHQ
BNZGVUBQ. - GTNHUG NGSIGSB

. . . .

178.

DOWPH HTERDTHA AVWPZ EUGS HE HTW
HTERDTHYRG BKUJ, XRH DOWPH PQHKEUA
AVWPZ HE PGG BPUZKUJ. - HTWEJEOW
OEEAWFWGH

. . . .

179.

XRR HGF UFMXDJ VXA VHDM KFGM SE OM
IXPM KIM VHGFXWM KH BGFJGM KIMD. -
OXRK USJAMN

. . . .

180.

DQAWA LN TB MRBTZ KLGA FAMWLTR MT
OTDBKP NDBWZ LTNLPA BY ZBO. - UMZM
MTRAKBO

. . . .

181.

YFKERMDQK SYJ'E ORZQ EY KEYL BYI. CG
BYI UIJ CJEY R NRDD, SYJ'E EIUJ RUYIJS
RJS VCZQ IL. - HCMORQD XYUSRJ

. . . .

182.

VCH'Q DLQ MSNQ ECY ONHHCQ VC ZHQLITLIL MZQS MSNQ ECY ONH VC. - GCSH MCCVLH

. . . .

183.

QPX ZXAU HP UEG UESWYA QPX UESWL QPX JNWWPU HP. - GCGNWPI IPPAGRGCU

. . . .

184.

DNM JQHM ZFVVFTAGD DNM CFTDQHB, DNM PHMRDMH DNM NREEFWMUU FW LFWWFWP. - EMGM

. . . .

185.

ZRIOB BLVGSZM TVMBSL BOVK MWJKF.

BORM RM HOE MWXS ASWAZS VAASVL

DLRIOB JKBRZ EWJ OSVL BOSX MASVY. -

VZVK FJKFSM

. . . .

186.

VQLS WLSSCZR WJRS KE TKHC KR JHSCE

KEMKRKOTC. - GFLEC CTXKE

. . . .

187.

R MXK'C WUSL CJUC CJLI ZCXVL OI RMLU.

R WUSL CJUC CJLI MXK'C JUQL UKI XG

CJLRS XPK. - KRHXVU CLZVU

. . . .

188.

EPM OIV AMFH KH EKRM XGKMH. EPM TBBV AMFH KH QBL'ZM EPM YKGBE. - RKDPIMG IGEHPLGMZ

. . . .

189.

AQVNZA ENO ZGO NOEAVT L ES VXZ VP AGEQO. L CEZIG ZGOS EBB VT ZU. - ZGVSEA AVCOBB

. . . .

190.

JAJFVODMLN VTE'AJ JAJF ZPLOJY MW TL ODJ TODJF WMYJ TC CJPF. - NJTFNJ PYYPMF

. . . .

191.

GXX TIVCIJOO FGYJO TXGHJ VNFOMEJ FAJ

HVRUVIF LVZJ. - RMHAGJX KVAZ PVPGY

. . . .

192.

QXNM LTQWR YTQ YZNN UZWD PQZXP LQQ

OVU BVX EQWWZGNM OZXF QJL TQY OVU

QXR BVX PQ. - L. W. RNZQL

. . . .

193.

AX NVZT VJ AOT UBUTJA AOVHD VH AOT

RXUNC. WXJA GTXGNT TFVJA, AOBA VJ

BNN. - XJKBU RVNCT

. . . .

194.

DNNG TYMKJGR, DNNG WNNZR, FJG F REKKQS UNJRUMKJUK, BCMR MR BCK MGKFE EMTK. - HFYZ BLFMJ

. . . .

195.

L HF EVD H WPVXGID VY FQ ILPIGFTDHEINT. L HF H WPVXGID VY FQ XNILTLVET. - TDNWKNE IVBNQ

. . . .

196.

VKL TESSLTTREI DCQQBXQ BT VKL CYLQCOL PCU, DBVK ICTLQ-IBJL RXSET. - GQESL ILL

. . . .

197.

NTHI TZEBHQUSC LQHNQL PFTC DSE
NTHIURT QFHQ IUGT UL PUIZ HCZ DSE JCSP
CSQFUCO HASEQ UQ. - YHVUYT IHOHBT

. . . .

198.

GUSO UB W RKQHNWUH. PKQF ZKWG UB NK
SUHX PKQF JWNM, HKN NK FOWTM NMO
NKJ. - RWIURO GWZWTO

. . . .

199.

SZH'NI WZY YZ WIY HB INILS UZLXFXW PFYV
TIYILUFXKYFZX FR SZH'LI WZFXW YZ WZ YZ
JIT PFYV MKYFMRKGYFZX. - WIZLWI
QZLFUIL

. . . .

200.

VPFM PYJBU TRPU JURMF AMJAKM URGDL PDC XJB TGKK PKTPXN YM URMGF AFGNJDMF. - KPJ UWB

. . . .

201.

Z ILLEZKJLF VX OJYYFOO LG LWZO. Z UFSFE CISF GE LGGQ IUX FTYJOF. - BHGEFUYF UZCWLZUCIHF

. . . .

202.

DCL VJD DJ RZQJKZ I KIV JT BFQQZBB RFD CIDUZC DJ RZQJKZ I KIV JT AINFZ. - INRZCD ZPVBDZPV

. . . .

203.

LBUDVNUDL   VPD   ZWDLVNBKL   RMD
EBUSGNERVDF RKF VPD RKLJDML RMD
LNUSGD. - FM. LDWLL

. . . .

204.

IKHYMUQHIQ MD 10 WQSIQHV BKSO ZHU 90
WQSIQHV UQTADMKH. - VMHZ YQP

. . . .

205.

WNANFI RJW CMOFVRY YUO PSYSMO. YUO
VFOJ VE YN UJHO J PVMG LMJEC NP YUO
CMOEOWY. - COYOM P. FMSRQOM

. . . .

206.

YSOUX   OR   Z   ICZUWCA   KDZB   QGSA
OAZXOUOUX. - MZGMZGZ RPDG

. . . .

207.

CYF YPSC SXNJ YPBJ, EFG XK CYF QY XG

AXDUG, YPBJ XZ JPYFDU. - VIJ LJZG

. . . .

208.

HCUIJK SVWN VOH XLKH ZVW HCVKL SCV

RENL HCL XLKH VZ CVS HCUIJK SVWN VOH.

- DVCI SVVYLI

. . . .

209.

IRG LDEG VDO TYDN NRD VDO PEG, PYW

NRPI VDO NPYI, IRG ZGJJ VDO ZGI IRKYHJ

OXJGI VDO. - JIGXRPYKG XGETKYJ

. . . .

210.

VMA CXVXQA PAJIDZU VI VMIUA SMI
PAJEAHA ED VMA PAWXVB IC VMAEQ
FQAWYU. - AJAWDIQ QIIUAHAJV

. . . .

211.

MDY KWN JDG SLEYLMYT MDY XSQVM
JDYYI JRV RL STSGM. MDY KWN JDG
SLEYLMYT MDY GMDYQ MDQYY JRV R
KYLSWV. - VST ORYVRQ

. . . .

212.

YBAD UNIBOCU QI DTHROGU BO
HIQHQILBQO LQ QOD'U WQVIRKD. - RORU
OBO

. . . .

213.

YC MCW UEPRI PU PO LDUUDX UC SQPV QU
OCTDUEPRA JCXUEJEPVD, CX OWNNDDY
QU OCTDUEPRA TDQRPRAVDOO. - UCTTM
JQVVQNE

. . . .

214.

KLD BER JPKR XENU YENBRUX YKB WE GEU
XEN, MNR JPKR XEN YKB WE GEU XENU
YENBRUX. - FEPB G. DVBBVWX

. . . .

215.

NS NVY'S PFZOZ UTA EHDZ IOTD. NS'V
PFZOZ UTA'OZ MTNYM SFHS ETAYSV. -
ZGGH INSRMZOHGK

. . . .

216.

GJJT YPPS KRZJ RNZDIP, NRY ZCPR UJD
OKGG DRYPIXZNRY PQPIUZCKRH VPZZPI. -
NGVPIZ PKRXZPKR

. . . .

217.

FG IMPACDFPH XISAAN TPXUO, ZPT KPBI
BPDZIXO PHAN ZSMI DTP ZSHYO? - BFADPH
VIXAI

. . . .

218.

JTZLF CQ ZTO OXL JTQO CJATMOYZO
OXCZS CZ OXL KTMIW. ITBL CQ.
GTMORZYOLIF, C ITBL JTZLF. - PYVDCL
JYQTZ

. . . .

219.

FDABDAS MYP BDXZI MYP JCZ, YS MYP JCZ'B, AXBDAS FCM MYP'SA SXUDB. - DAZSM TYSW

. . . .

220.

JPS AJCBJVON QEVOJ EI CRR CXPVSUSGSOJ VA ZSAVBS. - OCQERSEO PVRR

. . . .

221.

QA DACAXLVA KALXH QZUBA QA HUV. QA MIAXEMNA VZAN GS LEVUMC. - FX. ZACXS BUCR

. . . .

222.

DO CJM NPU FJS QDHHDFL SJ PDIT SZU

MIMNH, CJM QDHH ZNAU SJ IUSSHU OJP

SZU JPWDFNPC. - KDG PJZF

. . . .

223.

AV LXGV X SCICET ZJ AWXF AV TVF, ZYF AV

LXGV X SCPV ZJ AWXF AV TCIV. - ACEMFNE

BWYQBWCSS

. . . .

224.

RG SKH NXA LBWXY RC, SKH NXA LK RC. -

QXOC LRPAWS

. . . .

225.

FH MSKKSDW XI BQELSUSEH MJQX ZIA XJSDO ZIA JQRH XIVQZ UIL XJH KSUH XJQX ZIA MQDX XICILLIM. - DHSK BXLQABB

. . . .

226.

OPHPHWPO KVNK JQK SPKKDJS GVNK UQF GNJK DI IQHPKDHPI N GQJTPOMFB IKOQXP QM BFEX. - TNBND BNHN

. . . .

227.

R'Q CGO PLO CGWC'A DPC CP NRO ZGOL RC'A CRQO MPU QO CP NRO, AP JOC QO JRHO QS JRMO CGO ZWS R ZWLC CP. - YRQR GOLNURV

. . . .

228.

GS'A FIVW SR NDIS I JDVARC OFR CDQDV

YGQDA XJ. - NIND VXSF

. . . .

229.

HXHMJ YUF PR CIMF UR YUFJ YHF UFN

NPHR UR U RPFBKH IFH. - YUMOPF

SHPNHBBHM

. . . .

230.

UFMV I XFOCKJE FM WXWJE VWUWIC CK

JWZIFM NKDWUAR, IMV UFMV I VWUWIC FM

WXWJE XFOCKJE CK JWZIFM NAZPRW. -

KJJFM HKKVHIJV

. . . .

231.

JT AHY IGXQ VHOZQEJXU AHY'SZ XZSZL EGP, AHY OYVQ KZ IJCCJXU QH PH VHOZQEJXU AHY'SZ XZSZL PHXZ. - QEHOGV NZTTZLVHX

. . . .

232.

SWLZQYADT ZDEYE ODTSH. XLY YNST ED WDSE AKTDMQTZS. - EAM ZFQLE ODESM

. . . .

233.

XMUT MK KR KVRBD. M LREXW BZDVTB KMAC RAT KRAC DVZA MADTBJBTD DVT DVREKZAW. - SZIP XRAWRA

. . . .

234.

UKD FTWY UT LIJJDLL WOY UKD FTWY UT

HWQMIFD WFD WMPTLU DZWJUMV UKD

LWPD. - JTMQO F. YWXQL

. . . .

235.

XVSAIOL ZJSMZLB UX XYL BSSV, IAX,

YLUVPJR OUARYXLV, YAVVPLB UGUH. -

ILJNUTPJ DVUJZOPJ

. . . .

236.

ASM YKBU FCU YN NHKXHKD ASM BHEHAW

YN ASM JYWWHRBM HW RU DYHKD RMUYKX

ASME HKAY ASM HEJYWWHRBM. - CZASLZ

O. OBCZQM

. . . .

237.

AMDL MCH'B IVYFB DMHZMHP RYFNCLAD.

AMDL MC IVYFB GNLIBMHP RYFNCLAD. -

PLYNPL VLNHINZ CKIJ

. . . .

238.

MER MK LO HXMR NAI VA TMBGK M

VLOOGYGWEG. LR VAGK. - HLJJLMT CMTGK

. . . .

239.

FGFPK UJPYNF APYTQU HF IZBUFP JB JXF

TFVJ XBHF PMT. - AEAF PMJX

. . . .

240.

LIT'H HSYX DGMX HII CXOGINCDZ. ZIN'DD

TXQXO AXH INH IM GH SDGQX. - XDWXOH

ENWWSOL

241.

XAS FGWXIEKS OSXDSSE GEWIEGXN IEF CSEGJW GW VSIWJBSF ZEHN ON WJKKSWW. - OBJKS MSGBWXSGE

242.

KPABEIRGIS SDCKI ABK TDFUV. - GFABEF LGUWDEF

243.

SKJ'I SKAJTDWSH NKVD SDHWQ FVGI IK LRI NKVD DHWCRIN. VBTDWSH NKVD PKJERPIRKJ IK QWIPU NKVD SHGIRJN. - GIVWDI GPKII

244.

NQKFQJQ CHR VTU TUO CHR'MQ DTKESTC WDQMQ. - WDQHOHMQ MHHIQJQKW

. . . .

245.

EZD TAVNDX M NA HCASE TMRMVN, M ODD ME'O EZD XDTHEMAVOZML EZHE MO KAOE KDHVMVNYST. - UMTTMHK OZHEVDX

. . . .

246.

KYW UBDK FUXBMKQSK KYFSLD QMW KYW YQMNWDK KB DQO, JWAQPDW IBMND NFUFSFDY KYWU. - DKWXYWS TFSL

. . . .

247.

NMXH TLEU EK AQI GHILOEUS MR AQI

KQIVV AQLA IUWVMKIK NMXH

XUBIHKALUBEUS. - OLQVEV SEGHLU

. . . .

248.

NQOG MGIVIUC XDGXOTVCHUXIV ZQU'C

ZICIGTDUI EBIGI NQO XHU JQ. CBIN TIGIRN

ZICIGTDUI EBIGI NQO VCHGC. - UDZQ

AOPIDU

. . . .

249.

ABSSGAA FA DJE DFOD VJB ZJBKSG EDGK

VJB DFX ZJXXJC. - OGJTOG A. UMXXJK

. . . .

250.

RP RU HFQFZ PYY EDPF PY LF AXDP SYK GROXP XDQF LFFH. - OFYZOF FERYP

. . . .

251.

AHWC WCF ACC OGZFUA PA OGCN PVC PFJ APN MGN? Z JVCPW OGZFUA OGPO FCQCV MCVC PFJ APN MGN FHO. - UCHVUC DCVFPVJ AGPM

. . . .

252.

MKVMBQ HNRNRONH GWMG BTE MHN MOQTKEGNKB EFZAEN, LEQG KZIN NYNHBTFN NKQN. - RMHPMHNG RNMX

. . . .

253.

RU PVEJVH QIGT RT FMC RVKJWF JV BMGT, ZAJ LWTK M EVABPK'J XIU JWT ZMBB WT QIGT RT FMC RVKJWF RVHT. - LIBJTH RIJWIA

. . . .

254.

XBH QUD MDLDU IBB BCV IB NDI QMBIYDU TBQC BU IB VUDQS Q MDG VUDQS. - P.N. CDGAN

. . . .

255.

QLPQAL VP SPM AFHR JMGLSWMY, MYLN AFHR CTAA. - DTHMPG YOWP

. . . .

256.

SDHJ KDELPJQX OSS WGFEMX JUKJRW
RDHJQWV OEY WDDWGOKGJ. - ZOJ NJXW

. . . .

257.

CHPXJ JZNZQQZB BHJX JZMYK. - ICHSYRIJX
RYQQIJJ RQZBDHDP

. . . .

258.

VR GTJM HTR UBRRJN OTY MKTYKE ETW FT
MT KTHF BM ETW GT HTR MRTD. -
XTHLWXVWM

. . . .

259.

S OSJ IDN LKSJVL QNX JNKDBJR IBFF QSFF
QNX SJPKDBJR. - OSFENFO Z

260.

ZCR TCF'U QDJQZV FGGT Q YDQF.
VCNGUSNGV ZCR BRVU FGGT UC
AEGQUKG, UERVU, DGU XC QFT VGG JKQU
KQYYGFV. - NQFTZ KQDG

. . . .

261. GSA XUTO FHAEUD LFDEQSIA XUTO
AMUTZMA, XUTO JSGESQ FDK XUTO
BFIIEUD. - LUMFLLSK FGE JFBEO

. . . .

262.

RXIMARP ZAOO ZXFG KROHDD JXK VX. -
WTJT TRPHOXK

. . . .

263.

FG PSN ZSH'W TFXO RSDOWEFHB UELHBO
FW. FG PSN ULH'W UELHBO FW, UELHBO
WEO JLP PSN WEFHX LVSNW FW. - DLMP
OHBOTVMOFW

. . . .

264.

ZA AZH PGZ PANSHMH FBME DAC AZ QHBZY
DAC. NAKM AV RBVH BK G KHGXPE VAX FEA
GZI FEGM ZHHIK DAC MEH NAKM. - ZGOGR
XGOBLGZM

. . . .

265.

MDUUFZA   UFIFZ   ELDN,   KUS   ELDNNFZA
UFIFZ MDU. - IDUVF QTGXKZSD

. . . .

266.

BXBSU GCJ FGI ONBG HO'P VCCI OC POCR
KDHTYHGV FGI FRRSBKHFOB ONB XHBJ
ZSCT SHVNO JNBSB UCM FSB. - DCSH
IBPKNBGB

. . . .

267.

GYJA U WUA DSJAQ U TUX VDDX CDX YPQ
GPCJ, PR'Q JPRYJX U AJG TUX DX U AJG
GPCJ. - SXPATJ SYPFPS

. . . .

268.

GY VYF QY AKTWT FKT DNFK ENX BTNG, QY
JVHFTNG AKTWT FKTWT JH VY DNFK NVG
BTNRT N FWNJB. - WNBDK ANBGY TETWHYV

. . . .

269.

WCWN PNDWX. WCWN RKDZWX. FA
EKPPWN. PNI KBKDF. RKDZ KBKDF. RKDZ
OWPPWN. - UKEMWZ OWLYWPP

. . . .

270.

NK'W DPK RGAKGAJ ZPT YAK XDPHXAI
IPRD, NK'W RGAKGAJ ZPT YAK TO. - MNDHA
EPSFCJIN

. . . .

271.

JIU'Q RZEU QNK PIVOJ ZUJ OIWK LIGV
WIGO, PEWJIF EW YKQQKV QNZU WEOMKV
IV RIOJ. - YIY FZVOKL

. . . .

272.

JO KXG PT, DIX? JO KXG KXD, DIBK? - QXIK

O. EBKKBWM

. . . .

273.

LAUD   BWNVGXN   IKGBDAMJA   WE   QWOA

BWNVGXN DWJVN. - NVGCUE VXYDAP

. . . .

274.

SWT ZWCTY OEPNTV CP JCYT CU SWES

DMA QED SEGT SMM QEPD KVTZEASCMPU.

- EJYVTO EOJTV

. . . .

275.

MHTMVRMEYM RU EWJ BDKJ DKTTMEU JW

NWA, RJ'U BDKJ NWA ZW BRJD BDKJ

DKTTMEU JW NWA. - KXZWAU DAHXMN

98

. . . .

276.

K PVB XZVQRKY QEIJOIL ZVQR FOOC. K YER

EX GL YIOBKR YVIBQ. - POUUL LSEUJGVU

. . . .

277.

WTK WTKOEXUP, HE VKRC HE HDWGTSW

AD QCX XDQAOX KDAJXOEX, SXEXOJX

WTKO UTJX HDS HPPXRQATD. - GKSSCH

. . . .

278.

KBVYBEY FK KFIIFEW FE ILY KLGJY IBJGZ

QYTGCKY KBVYBEY DAGEIYJ G IMYY G

ABEW IFVY GWB. - UGMMYE QCSSYII

. . . .

279.

HU MHUC HO I DHLCR KIAC, XTC KYIGTHFO IYC KYCIX, JSX XTC GMRX HO FRVUSOHVK IVL XTC XSXRYHIM HO PIE XRR MRVK. - CMRV ASOQ

. . . .

280.

KCGUKB HNR BRS GUK LZH, NB GUK LZH BRSP HNR. - FCX BNUS

. . . .

281.

IYAW DYRWQN QK ICKWQ, EKW'D QK IRDY DYAT. - AZBRN VCANZAO

. . . .

282.

AKS MOFRGT GM ODMS DW GY AKS SUVS. - YFRFO TFRDNFYA

. . . .

283.

BKRM JOWU TGW DN NOCPNM BKRM
SMOFKW KM BKRM SGYGTN. VPGC BKR
JGXN OC OF BKRMF CK UNTOUN -
DNMWGMU XNYQOW TYOQN

. . . .

284.

JFTQ FR IAQ TJPDQX TPX DAFYA JPHQ FR
IAQ APLQO. - HFYIPX ACNP

. . . .

285.

L FLWT BO L CKLDM PRLP VBKK KMWX INQ
ZNWMI BU INQ DLW CHNEM PRLP INQ XNW'P
WMMX BP. - FNF RNCM

. . . .

286.

VXIRQ RD TP FUE'KK KTAI PUXIAIX, KTAI RD TP FUE'KK VTI JUVRF. - HRQID VIRG

. . . .

287.

S PRJKQ UEQ HEN P ZSJK, ZFY S JCEL UEQ QEKRC'Y LENJ YMPY LPO. RE S RYEIK P ZSJK PCQ PRJKQ HEN HENUSAKCKRR. - KWE TMSISTR

. . . .

288.

E VNXX UPI, EM VBED TPHXS YNEMC K XEVVXN JHKLU BNXZD VP QNNZ UPI DKMN. - LDK LDK CKYPH

. . . .

289.

J OCV'I IDJVR CL SWW IDM NJUMAX PFI CL IDM PMSFIX IDSI UIJWW AMNSJVU. - SVVM LASVR

. . . .

290.

HBTHQB LCT DEB NEDMG BITPJC YT YCXIW YCBG NDI NCDIJB YCB LTEQS, DEB YCB TIBA LCT ST. - ETU AXQYDIBI

. . . .

291.

HFEBUF QE EQT WOQ UE POWV OQS XOVT O PNOQS QTA IHONH, OQCEQT WOQ IHONH ZNEX QEA OQS XOVT O PNOQS QTA TQSLQU. - WONK PONS

. . . .

292.

LZZ FENRU QIQFGTAQ, ZEAQ OY LZYRLPQUEHLZZG LHHTFWEAN UT GTOF RQENRU. - HLCQG CUQANQZ

. . . .

293.

YASL E TFA TNFAPI XL SEUI. AY YAI TFA BY EZ UYW XI. - TFWYS RGWAIZZ

. . . .

294.

DOCH OA JZW YEZBW COJNOJS KZBPAHDC. DOCH OA YEZBW FPHYWOJS KZBPAHDC. - DZDDK NYALYD

. . . .

295.

WKH FBKN ULSNH, OTGI, SGI MBKZ TGHB
LDLG FBKN MOSZZLMH SJHM. HUTM TM HUL
MLJNLH BR MKJJLMM. - MASOT MTDSGSGIS

. . . .

296.

ZMH VHQO XIIXVZLJEZR PXV CLFFHCC
OEHC NEZMEJ ZMH IHVCXJ QJY JXZ EJ ZMH
BXD. - TEA TEAOQV

. . . .

297.

NUTYU MPBYB AKI TYB. INB MPTU AKI PTQB.
LK MPTU AKI STE. - TYUPIY TNPB

. . . .

298.

WPC HVWVXC ECNMBYJ WM WPMJC GPM
KXCKRXC HMX ZW WMLRD. - ARNSMNA U

. . . .

299.

XV JBR GKLGDY BK ADKV. XVADVFV ROGR

ADKV DI MBLRO ADFDJE, GJY CBQL XVADVK

MDAA   OVAN   WLVGRV   ROV   KGWR.   -

MDAADGU PGUVI

. . . .

300.

DALT'W   EII   CZWETPAIGW   EI   EFHT   EII

WTPAIGW. - CFPZ TRXTDMPTAE

. . . .

301.

EZGM   EN   GJZANRN   AYEGHODT   EADD

JZGYCN LPMNH HNGDAMT. - IDPMGHJZ

. . . .

302.

RVSG VF RVPG LVYVUJ H CVZXZRG. MT
PGGO XTKL CHRHUZG, XTK DKFM PGGO
DTBVUJ. - HRCGLM GVUFMGVU

. . . .

303.

FW ZGYC IW FKEEKTA CR EWC AR RM CLW
EKMW FW NEJTTWQ YR JY CR LJOW CLW
EKMW CLJC KY FJKCKTA MRB GY. - HRYWNL
PJZNIWEE

. . . .

304.

LDO LDAYKDLIYJ UAYJ LA UAJMLYZO
QOLMQOU. - AGXQ SDXNNXG

. . . .

305.

ZH OFWM FX ZH ZMXXIEM. - ZIBIRZI EIPGBF

. . . .

306.

LBS ISPL LBMJX ZITHL LBS EHLHNS MP LBZL

ML GTDSP TJS VZR ZL Z LMDS. - ZINZBZD

AMJGTAJ

. . . .

307.

DR SJI OQTP PJ NDRP SJIULWNR IE, NDRP

IE   LJVWJTW   WNLW.   -   XJJFWU   P.

OQLADTKPJT

. . . .

308.

IXFV FV MBQN ZFEH OYK FI'V HYKFYT BYH

GFYQIH OI O IFGH. - IMZHN KQNKHY

309.

QT Q RMAJZ GX IQGAJX'T GPDF RLDTATHPZ LI HNL RMLARPT, HQOP AH LW JPQCP AH. - KFZZX MQROPHH

310.

ZJZKUHJO KG KVU EHFJO, KG KVU AKUWO LQC KVU CJJCO AHEE MKQDHQVJ HQ KDIJUO. - UKOL XLUWO

311.

NOEGMQLUS LR VNMXSLSY PTMQ CUE OLOS'Q NANS JSUP CUE OLOS'Q JSUP. - OMSLNV H. KUUXRQLS

312.

M LMG DCSOFAS IMAJOSUW CK M LMG

DMKSUL. - ZOMWICU ZOMTICX

. . . .

313.

XBBA EDRIRFY, TBJHVEB IRQB RE H

TBHVORQVI OGRFY HFS OGBKB'E EP DVJG

OP EDRIB HTPVO. - DHKRIWF DPFKPB

. . . .

314.

ZH VRW BPSQQV QRRJ KQRTPQV, URTG

RMPBAZFEG TWKKPTTPT GRRJ S QRAF

GZUP. - TGPMP YRCT

. . . .

315.

RPP PBGQ BZ RT QKSQOBAQTC. CWQ AIOQ QKSQOBAQTCZ JIN ARVQ CWQ UQCCQO. - ORPSW FRPHI QAQOZIT

. . . .

316.

JHDE CHODR VAZAELSIAR JHDE EAUXSZJ. - MAHEMA XDOUR

. . . .

317.

BJM UKB JVXB RMFFPPG AT BJM GPRAHP RMFFPPGAVC. BJM UKB JVXB TKAX AT BJM GJ VJI UAVG TKAXAVC. - EYAXAEEJR

. . . .

318.

ASN   DTHNDZ   VNXTRN   NUASNO

ASTGESAPGD TO NRLAZ. - RYJTH XTTDNZ

. . . .

319.

OFQTRU   YOV   URQ   ONDOVW   CLTUX

KOEETUBWW   CMQ   QKBLB   TW   UR

KOEETUBWW   DTQKRMQ   OFQTRU.   -

CBUAOYTU ZTWLOBNT

. . . .

320.

R TNIIMTTCNO HRU FT VUM EDV IRU ORW R

CFKH   CVNUZRYFVU   EFYD   YDM   JKFIQT

VYDMKT DRXM YDKVEU RY DFH. - ZRXFZ

JKFUQOMW

. . . .

321.

MQL FLNEO FQLFMGO NP ZKNG UNHO NG ZM KOUF MZKOLG. CPT NH JMQ ACP'Z KOUF ZKOE, CZ UOCGZ TMP'Z KQLZ ZKOE. - TCUCN UCEC

. . . .

322.

GE KQT EGPC GS RYIC SQ VYTUR YS KQTIJBVE, G HQTVC OB RYLLK SQ CQ GS EQI KQT. - UIQTZRQ WYIM

. . . .

323.

ASZ AKIPZXH GD JGMZ XTZWD'A JGZ GD DTA KZIUSGDP HTOK PTIJ. ASZ AKIPZXH JGZW GD SICGDP DT PTIJ AT KZIUS. - RZDNIFGD FIHW

113

. . . .

324.

XTRJ TV YZZ TNIZUYMQY YZ EJ YMHJQ

VJUTZDVXL. - ZVPMU GTXKJ

. . . .

325.

XQZ SJLLZYZKBZ MZXVZZK AXWGJSJXR

PKS NZKJWA JA XQPX NZKJWA QPA JXA

EJTJXA. - PEMZYX ZJKAXZJK

. . . .

326.

WOU DHCUWUV QMH GUYMBU, WOU BMVU

QMH KVU KGNU WM OUKV. - VHBC

. . . .

327.

CLVMAFVMC XLG PFKK JMQMB TJLP AEM

QYKGM LO Y VLVMJA, GJAFK FA ZMRLVMC

Y VMVLBX. - HB. CMGCC

. . . .

328.

ZP JVE IRZYQ YVMVWJ GHKCX ZP JVE'KC

HOZUC, IKJ AZXXZYD H GVETOC VP GHK

THJACYIX. - CHKO SZOXVY

. . . .

329.

C GECZTLG EA ZYSYMV C MIZR TN XTCM

DKCD GEG QYMM ILGYS RSYAAISY. -

ILULTQL

. . . .

330.

BYN XEPL IY TLL VECONML ET IXL GLHCUUCUH EUF IXL ZCFFOL, GNI ULPLM LUILMIECU CI ET EU LUF. - ALTTCKE XLMMCU

. . . .

331.

DYKXMFE YVJBD TBGMN MG KMXW HYFNMFE YVJBD YONCMDWNDBOW. - GDWIW TYODMF

. . . .

332.

OFU SFD MFOX, KTU SFD DCMM GFT SBRC MWRCP WY USC NBWO USWOX. - YCOCLB

. . . .

333.

EJM'N PCSME NVLS RSBNVMZ JM B YBTT,
DJCVMZ NJ NUBMPOJUL VN VMNJ B EJJU. -
HJHJ HDBMST

. . . .

334.

TMHGQC NR PMC BHY LJ BNJC. PMLRC YML
BLLO LGBX PL PMC EHRP LU EUCRCGP HUC
TCUPHNG PL VNRR PMC JWPWUC. - KLMG J.
OCGGCIX

. . . .

335.

WSX XYLYP WSBY SXR WSOYPVSZ SK
PYKVZVYXO SK ODY DHWSX KEVPVO. -
QYPX JVZZVSWK

. . . .

336.

WJFLMSFLW ZJQ YSV, WJFLMSFLW ZJQ
XLHGV. - BJAV E. FHDYLXX

. . . .

337.

IFYEHFX EPBZ WJDZ TM AYFM AYMD BEBN
EHZP VMBS. - SYDB UBSID

. . . .

338.

QU'K UVXG OZVP YBVH FGCGV HQDDGP
ZFJABPJ, AXU Q MQIXVG, YOJ UZHG UOG
EOZFEG? - VBFZDP VGZIZF

. . . .

339.

CKDB CKQB LG LPB QJCCBIL, EAO QGZJI GA
LPB YGIKLKDB. - UELL ZEUBHGA

. . . .

340.

SIP HIJ'W NQCG WI EGG WNG VNIYG

EWQZARQEG, TPEW WQXG WNG LZAEW

EWGF. - KQAWZJ YPWNGA XZJM TA

. . . .

341.

MQC DNZ SWOZ MQC DVTN. - KNEEVXNB

UQINR

. . . .

342.

REZT EW MKI Q VYKARTB IK AT WKRPTF,

ACI Q YTQREIN IK AT TLVTYETMGTF. -

WKYTM UETYUTXQQYF

. . . .

343.

JFAR XLFXHL FZLMLARQJPRL VNPR RNLS
DPU WF QU FUL SLPM PUW
CUWLMLARQJPRL VNPR RNLS DPU WF QU
RLU SLPMA. - IQHH TPRLA

. . . .

344.

YMMU GNLB ZEPM DN DXM HLRHXJRM ERV
GNL PERRND HMM E HXEVNK. - XMQMR
YMQQMB

. . . .

345.

VX GMIQX, PAGP JK PAX KXWDXP IY
JQFXQPJIQ. VX GMIQX, PAGP JK SAXQ
JRXGK GDX VIDQ. - QJNIMG PXKMG

. . . .

346.

NR IRD XGD YAFD JRZ QFIIRD NR SIDGUBGUG YSDA YAFD JRZ QFI NR. - KRAI YRRNGI

. . . .

347.

LZ Y FAZQTA NYI, IUJ MYZ OKYBA QKA NUWTG. - SYKYQSY FYZGKL

. . . .

348.

WELV EK U TMVKSERB UBX NRJ JV WEFV ES EK RMQ UBKJVQ. - PUQZ IVWWVQ

. . . .

349.

ENVYMZX JT, IJAM ZXICB ENQZ, AWNEZ
WCDZ, EUJVY WCDZ, UXL LCX'M VZM AC
OCDRZL JT UPCJM MYNXVA. - RZXXZMY
PDUXUVY

. . . .

350.

KGT ICTUIZT QFZ PN I XPYTU BTUNFX KGIX
KGT ICTUIZT BTUNFX. - IXQA UFFXTA

. . . .

351.

ULKQ LW CJJ IQQG KJN VJNIW, WJ IJX'C
CND CJ IQWENLZQ LC, FYWC ULAQ LC. - E.
W. UQVLW

. . . .

352.

WNHT NO YZUJ. ZHQTU ZWW, NQ INWWO ECR. - IZQYZUNXT YTBKRUX

. . . .

353.

O FKSEG WHZALW GOL KQ VHRROKP ZAHP KQ CKWLGKN. - UOPDLPZ UHP BKBA

. . . .

354.

MBGGBQXPD IWM VZIWBWLGXP JBPP IPJIOA UYBWL VHYZ AIDBAGIQDBHW DCIW ZIAO IWM VZIWBWLPZAA. - VIFBVZ PILIQZ

. . . .

355.

GOTCT XCT GLU LXRQ UN QSCTXPYJK VYKOG. GU ET GOT DXJPVT, UC GOT WYCCUC GOXG CTNVTDGQ YG. - TPYGO LOXCGUJ

. . . .

356.

UFV CPHX MRADORHRUX RP HRWV RA D ODM DUURUEMV. - AICUU FDQRHUCP

. . . .

357.

QK LUIIW JTZ CLGR BTBKYC. CLGR BTBKYC GR WTEZ HGJK. - TBUZ VLUWWUB

. . . .

358.

Q'C WFTWRL VMQIA KDQIAL Q XWI'K VM.
KDWK'L DMT Q ASK KM VM KDSC. - ZWEFM
ZQXWLLM

. . . .

359.

MR UF WFFY PTRK DQB'P AWBFGR KFO. -
UPRCR XQGPAB

. . . .

360.

HGKA RZQ LIA MR KWGPIFPSL RZQO LZKVY
PY SZA KY PCEZOAKSA KY HGKA RZQ
MIWZCI MR KWGPIFPSL RZQO LZKVY. - NPL
NPLVKO

. . . .

361.

LMLOS   PJHRL   EJOA   FX   VC   KFOXC

FNBJXXFHRL. - CYJNVX TVORSRL

. . . .

362.

ICKP BQVID CV KUPCNMUA CNKC ZKWDI

PVY AQKX PVY KLD KQMOD. - NKHDG

. . . .

363.

HT OVP PTX, HO'N TQO OVP SPLFN HT SQIF

AHYP OVLO GQITO. HO'N OVP AHYP HT SQIF

SPLFN. - LUFLVLD AHTGQAT

. . . .

364.

XNKNE IC WCRCEECP PJFW DCG HFX IC

WCIFD.   UECHEFYWLXFWLCX   LY   WJN

WJLNQ CQ WLRN. - HJFEZNY ILHONXY

. . . .

365.

CI RPL'KN PIINKNB T QNTA PD T KPMUNA QWCF, BPD'A TQU HWTA QNTA, VLQA YNA PD. - QWNKRE QTDBGNKY

. . . .

366.

FAS UQGV LOQCDY CD FASO UVQB. FAS UQGV RVVE CD FASO YUAVY. FAS NQD YEVVO FASOYVKR QDF BCOVNECAD FAS NUAAYV. - BO. YVSYY

. . . .

367.

KIBHANAD HIA ZLPT FX ZBP WBP WFPWALNA BPT RAULANA, LH WBP BWILANA. - PBJFUAFP ILUU

. . . .

368.

RFG UKPZ QVMUXXQLPG WUOCKGZ QX
RFG UKG ZUO KGTGC LGIQK. - RUKZ
CULLQKX

. . . .

369.

OSY GFEY DRLROYMMLUYRO Q GQR LB,
OSY MYBB GVBOYELFDB YNLBOYRIY
BYYGB OF SLG. - QEOSDE BISFZYRSQDYE

. . . .

370.

RMGG ZLTM HA YMJJMD JBQT RMGG AQHZ.
- YMTPQCHT KDQTXGHT

. . . .

371.

ZMB KIBUZBXZ KWFIJ HR WHEHRK WHBX

RFZ HR RBEBI TUWWHRK, ACZ HR IHXHRK

BEBIJ ZHVB GB TUWW. - RBWXFR VURPBWU

. . . .

372.

YH EYHW JWPW FPWTYMAICEW YA JQBET

MWIUW AQ CW EYHW, IRT CW JYALQBA

HEISQP. - WEWIRQP PQQUWSWEA

. . . .

373.

DNT YLOMZ PMALX SD MXC SKM CFG RM

PMWDQM ZLYMXS FPDNS SKLXAZ SKFS

QFSSMT. - QFTSLX YNSKMT ULXA IT

. . . .

374.

MZWRD'H   REEZLITPHNLVSMH   AVBV

DVHMVBWRD'H   PLIZHHPCPTPMPVH.   -

BZCVBM N. HENGTTVB

. . . .

375.

TOKD OMZ'N P VPNNDL CK VOTDMNCZDM,

JXN CK VCVDZNM. - LCMD EDZZDYR

. . . .

376.

MVDAD   LW   ZKAD   MK   HLPD   MVOS

LSBADOWLSN   LMW   WCDDU.   -   ZOVOMZO

NOSUVL

. . . .

377.

QPND BQO'ID KNNDAGDC BQOE VHKMY, PQ QPD NKP OYD GZDF KSKTPYG BQO. - SDQESD E.E. FKEGTP

. . . .

378.

JRR RWJYU BY YUGRA JQY SRHWRLJ RW REXUXRU BXJQRTJ JQY ZXFSRHWRLJ RW JQRTMQJ. - GRQU W. NYUUYZA

. . . .

379.

OGU EUHO SDB OQ OUDMG BQLT RXJH DEQLO ODZUH XH EB UDOXYC 30 VUTMUYO QI OGUXT XMU MTUDW. - EXFF WLTTDB

. . . .

380.

BVWG X WMDO WMCOH DBP BFAOPY MY X

WMDO   QBPFAQAMWO.   -   XWUOPF

OMVYFOMV

. . . .

381.

YPM YX HD I PIQAHXE QA KXWDXAD DTKD'K

LTXJV. - WIMI IAODTXJ

. . . .

382.

TPXGPNWSQB   SI   LQXSBR.   RPWWSBR

LPWWPX SI EZPXP UHH WZP GKB SI. -

YXURQI XQKU

. . . .

383.

PT VQY SWHYPHWZV MNHJ GQKWJAPHS,
RQH'J MNPJ TQE PJ. JWNIA VQYEGWZT JQ
OW PKLNJPWHJ. - SYEONDGA IANANZ

. . . .

384.

MXOOXJ   G   RJWXF   OJWOP   OPGZ   G
RTEITJOGMFX   BXFWQHTZ.   -   XBAGJB
GMMXK

. . . .

385.

OD XWEK RDZ WELI KD OD ZMKQF RDZ BEM
OD XWEK RDZ XEMK KD OD. - DAUEW
XQMPUIR

. . . .

386.

HPEBXRTX FBEI KOPVV NXEPBVK OPDXK
HXGSXTE P VPGUX FCGD, VBDX EIX
LRBZXGKX. - GLOB

. . . .

387.

KOKPXBTQDJ QM LSDDX, CM FHDJ CM QB'M
TCIIKDQDJ BH MHWKAHEX KFMK. - UQFF
PHJKPM

. . . .

388.

ITMUSUGL VFTVJF PITM AKF VODEF TH
FXFOGAKDIR UIS AKF XUJQF TH ITAKDIR. -
TLEUO MDJSF

. . . .

389.

ZDJA UZFVTP BYVL WKGZ LAZKF WKIZ DV D

BTHZW ITF TLAZFV. - FTVD UDFRV

. . . .

390.

AMIYGW   XAJQASG   TH   VEQQAVV   MV

VYTBMSI EX. - BTTFW DKKAS

. . . .

391.

PCGH   CU   L   UNBBHUUCMV   MG   PHUUMVU

IACBA   ENUS   QH   PCYHJ   SM   QH

NVJHKUSMMJ. - KLPWA ILPJM HEHKUMV

. . . .

392.

YAX YJIYA WN, XDXJBTLX WN ZTWLZ YT

AIJY BTI. BTI KINY ZTY YT EWLM YAX TLXN

FTJYA NIEEXJWLZ ETJ. - OTO CPJHXB

. . . .

393.

DEA LFW BD OAAX HDHAEBKH VDZEV ZG BD YFNA IDEGBFEBSW VJAFBAJ VDFSG. - HZIYFAS ODJMF

. . . .

394.

CN HAM DIFRX SAA JMBV SCJF SVCRUCRP WGAMS W SVCRP, HAM'EE RFZFY PFS CS XARF. - GYMBF EFF

. . . .

395.

SVL DMTE BTFGL ZVLXL OKGGLOO GDULO CLRDXL ZDXW PO PM SVL HPGSPDMFXE. - YPHFT OFOODDM

. . . .

396.

UYW'E CHLT EVT QJDT NTJI 75 EHDTQ JWU

SJCC HE J CHXT. - IYKHW QVJIDJ

. . . .

397.

FUW OVN NBUWAC LWIK OI FUW OVN. -

ENACOB EOVMDN

. . . .

398.

BGRHHXDOXW, ARKHTZXW, LXAXRQW RDL

THQKYRQXHS, IZEOZXWW, RZX FGRQ YRVX

SETZ   HKAX   FEZQGFGKHX.   -   YRPKYX

HRORBX

. . . .

399.

RMAD MN OSZD GA DCDY NG OSWU ISYKMWFN TDRZDZ KGFDKBDY. - VBSYRDN ZMVEDWN

. . . .

400.

HTNV VSJA ESO SI TG OZFY HTGV ASE MFIU KVQFL. - MZASLL RZHGQSLQ NZL QZVUAV

. . . .

401.

JSH UAMB RYPYFJ ZG JSH UAMB KBYFJ. - MHSXQSF VYFJ

. . . .

402.

ORMMRW MI WRLQUY TUDRYM QYP OR MBIHVBM Q NIID MBQY MI TGRQE IHM QYP WRLICR QDD PIHOM. - QOWQBQL DUYZIDY

. . . .

403.

AUD RDOA JPC AL FDA OAPIADK XO AL

HWXA APSBXTF PTK RDFXT KLXTF. - JPSA

KXOTDC

. . . .

404.

YG PQN WYJJAN HI S JYIIYMLAPK AYNC

HEEHTPLGYPK. - SADNTP NYGCPNYG

. . . .

405.

JCGY CO OXWVA, IKU CA CO BZ AW NWB AW

RIPY CA OTYYA. - OIVIX JWBCOY UYJIKN

. . . .

406.

FG'I XEG GQNG F'A IE IANUG, FG'I OKIG GQNG F IGNH PFGQ RUEJMVAI MEXCVU. - NMJVUG VFXIGVFX

. . . .

407.

AD KYM EFU ACFIAUW AZ, KYM EFU FEQAWPW AZ. AD KYM EFU RNWFC AZ, KYM EFU HWEYCW AZ. - SAJJAFC FNZQMN SFNR

. . . .

408.

OSY LKXH KU YRYPJOSKXW. VSBO JMG OSKXT JMG FYZMLY. - FGHHSB

. . . .

409.

IURSMAG RN ZEG WHQCRKGQZ ZEUZ PRTGN NMWWGNN RZ'N ISUTHA. - ZAMKUQ WUJHZG

. . . .

410.

NFGGNW AFLJE STW GSAWJ SLJ EYCJYWJ CB AFEVHTGYLW CYG ZTWSG AFLJE TFEW SCHRW FG. - KSEQFLZGHL FTRFLZ

. . . .

411.

UORMYW EKPA TXNW HKVRE. VKM'H YRDITW KM HOW NPHPAW, RUH MKC, CXHOKPH VWTRE. - ZXDKMW VW IWRPBKXA

. . . .

412.

PS TWFA CZSFSHSL BINNWPRS. WE WN DRCDON BINNWPRS. - ADRDW RDXD

. . . .

413.

HZFCF OL VRYT VRF XMT HV MBVOK QCOHOQOLI. KV RVHZORS, LMT RVHZORS, MRK AF RVHZORS. - MCOLHVHYF

. . . .

414.

YIYKUTVY GAEVLW TX NADVHEVH GAY STKJR, QZG VT TVY GAEVLW TX NADVHEVH AEBWYJX. - JYT GTJWGTU

. . . .

415.

P APHSPDU DY YTVWMRDUS ITC LTU'M
UWWL PM P KHDGW ITC GPU'M HWYDYM. -
BHPUNZDU OTUWY

. . . .

416.

N DYYS CEUQIP EUTPZSD CY OZ VUPZ,
OWC N VUPZ TNQ IQYVP EUTPZSD CY OZ N
DYYS. - VUSSUNT PENIZPRZNGZ

. . . .

417.

ZBWH BA MHIZZR ABQLZH, FSP EH BDABAP
CD QIUBDT BP JCQLZBJIPHY. - JCDWSJBSA

. . . .

418.

PRRPELSMTLTIB   JPM'L   OVRRIM,   UPS
WEIVLI LOIA. - WOETB FEPBBIE

419.

IBEBA TBIX NDFA VBGX. GQZGNM VDQX WH VWOV. QDDP HVB ZDAQX MHAGWOVH WI HVB BNB. - VBQBI PBQQBA

420.

KAUBDBV HRFP LUXBN ERX'C MTN ARQQFXBHH PFPX'C ZXUK KABVB CU HAUQ. - JBVCVTPB HCBFX

421.

LIN BADWZNF AV C LIADHCZP GQRNH MNOQZH KQLI AZN HLNS. - RCA LYD

422.

IFAU FB YLO G TGOOUK LA WLIZFYM MLLZ

NGKZB, EXO LA JIGHFYM G JLLK WGYZ DUII.

- KLEUKO ILXFB BOUSUYBLY

. . . .

423.

XTR   IRWY   BWF   FRORK   PGKHJOR.

PGKHJORFRLL JL XTR WXXKJNSXR GP XTR

LXKGFH. - QWTWXQW HWFETJ

. . . .

424.

ZKLNSGE NMGETH ZSNZM JWAL KJK, YAN

DALHAK WECJ NMWHK NMSN ZSDNALK NMK

MKSLN. - SEZGKEN GEFGSE DLWRKLY

. . . .

425.

HQK BASJ HQYAL HQEH YAHKCTKCKZ IYHQ

NJ SKECAYAL YZ NJ KPRXEHYBA. - ESFKCH

KYAZHKYA

. . . .

426.

UYV IEOOVNU JQFVHURGV KCR PJH VFVG

UJDV EN UC AEFV UYV AEBV CB KCRG

QGVJTN. - CXGJY SEHBGVK

. . . .

427.

FRNA RM ARDWAZ C ECZRJT CEOAJDKZA

XZ JXDWRJT CD CFF. - WAFAJ QAFFAZ

. . . .

428.

ARDRJM YZA BR DZYS ZAJ WEZCE Z AHL

DHBFAAFAB, DQE ZAMRAH YZA WEZCE

ERJZM ZAJ TZSH Z AHL HAJFAB. - TZCFZ

CRDFAWRA

. . . .

429.

KVZZXKK ZALXK TSAL BUOMYH GSXULK

EBUE USX WMHHXS EBUY QAVS TXUSK. -

WAWWQ VYKXS

. . . .

430.

XVYJL VW RFG MVJNWGC, WVR RFG

KGLRBWDRBVW. MVC BL XVJWK WVR BW

XBWBLFBWO DW DYRBUBRC SJR BW

KVBWO BR. - ONGO DWKGNLVW

431.

UF IFOTBHLOVSZ BO VCL HBYLIVBFO FT

ZFAY HYLNWD. SBGL VCL SBTL ZFA'GL

BWNUBOLH. - CLOYZ HNGBH VCFYLNA

. . . .

432.

EM E FDQQKW RK JUVDW WYEQJB, E FDQ

RK BNDOO WYEQJB EQ D JUVDW IDL. -

NDUWEQ OHWYVU GEQJ AU

. . . .

433.

LU ESV GVBBJWHJB FS FQJ TLWH, ESV

MYW BLHJ LF. - FSWL ZSBBLGSW

. . . .

434.

ZHOY XQEPUYV IYBF GJHXCZF, HP E IYBF

TNVHDHIY MEF, HO FNJ ZYD HD. - ZHPAVYF

INPP

. . . .

435.

VH MHPUZH VQIF VH FQXSJ IMULF ZUGF UO

FQH FXZH, ISC FQIF'G FQH GFAISDHGF

GHPAHF. - HIAB SXDQFXSDIBH

. . . .

436.

BCA DSV DCEGTSOV FRDSAKR YCKRK

LSMR XLCYVK, CY BCA DSV YRWCODR

FRDSAKR XLCYVK LSMR YCKRK. - XCE

JOTKCV

. . . .

437.

EO'D FEBT OY XT EALYPOUFO, XRO EO'D UJDY EALYPOUFO OY XT FEBT. FTZTP GYPQTO OWUO. - DUBWU XUPYF BYWTF

. . . .

438.

FXDXDNXF, ITLEP BY IRX ITDTFFTJ PTW JTFFBXL ENTWI PXYIXFLEP. - LEVX GEFSXKBX

. . . .

439.

EFCEWD PT GTT AEO, HRNEKDR GXEG'D CXROR WTK'FF AUBZ GXR GOKGX. - EFHROG NEYKD

. . . .

440.

BJ SRG SQCYJ KNJ GSIH KC NRK KNJ GSIH.

- ISWLN BSWMC JGJIVCP

. . . .

441.

J HGIHKQ HPPJEX GHCX HC CLX VAAJUX,

STC J FHOX TY AVP JC SK GXHEJBD XHPGK.

- ULHPGXQ GHFS

. . . .

442.

T CNFQ BL ILA KCB BZF TUF UCKFN PFXB

JRHHTVA LCB LJ YD AHRNN. - QRMTQ HFF

GLBZ

. . . .

443.

MVQ BZF FHIHT BTVDD NRH VBHZF QFNEU
MVQ RZIH NRH BVQTZYH NV UVDH DEYRN
VJ   NRH   DRVTH.   -   BRTEDNVARHT
BVUQXSQD

. . . .

444.

LY WKI IYN, LW'M YCW WKI PIFGM LY PCDG
SLTI WKFW VCDYW. LW'M WKI SLTI LY PCDG
PIFGM. - FXGFKFQ SLYVCSY

. . . .

445.

BTM'P XTKKS GUTJP YGZWJKRA, XTKKS
GUTJP PCR LCGMLRA STJ QZAA XCRM STJ
BTM'P RIRM PKS. - DGLE LGMYZRWB

. . . .

446.

WMZKVR MUMAO FYPPMFFIYX DLV KF L

FYAJAKFMR DBNZMA KV XLT. - UBXNLKAM

. . . .

447.

GEV GNQOP QJ YQCV QZ YVWNJQJU EKB

GK LVWY BQGE QG. - EVYVJ TQNNVJ

. . . .

448.

UIUQPZWU GSL S KAQKZLU NW RNBU.

KUQGSKL   PZAQL   NL   DSCXGNWM

CURUINLNZW. - TSINT RUCCUQYSW

. . . .

449.

MCA KXRRAWADLA OAMQAAD MCA XYNHIIXOTA GDK MCA NHIIXOTA TXAI XD G NAWIHD'I KAMAWYXDGMXHD. - MHYYB TGIHWKG

. . . .

450.

JG ZIM'D KGES GUGXFQMG, WPD GUGXFQMG ZIM KGES CQVGQMG. - XQMIEB XGIYIM

. . . .

451.

QC IBDPBXP PKIP QI RGSQXV CBU QE, CBBJ HOIE EGIEPI G KBE YPEEPU. - VQKYPUE VBEECUQPJ

. . . .

452.

S TSDY JXSHSJSGQ. SH QZDYG UNO

GHXNBL. - TYRXNB MZQYG

. . . .

453.

JEJOC AFSLM TFA F VFAM, FLX JEJOC

ASLLJO TFA F QGMGOJ. - KAPFO RSWXJ

. . . .

454.

YFFO KXWL DCQF CISCKV AXSCLH AMF

VWEVMJEF, CEH VMCHXSV SJII DCII

UFMJEH KXW. - SCIA SMJARCE

. . . .

455.

SE FEA MDGA AE RAYGNI AGKK API GYEF

GR PEA WOA VDNI GA PEA WB RAYGNGFZ. -

MGKKGDV WOAKIY BIDAR

456.

JUX RNHH IYPC AYBJ WCICYOV NB HNIC,
GXO BCZCF HCO JUXFVCHI GC WCICYOCW.
- AYJY YBTCHUX

457.

KWSWZ HLB VJJ BYII BVRVZZVA AXDB CVL
EDK MV BXW MDC DJBWZ BVRVZZVA. -
RDZQ BADYK

458.

XKRA KB MCJP CJUUALB MCAL QWD'SA
ZDBQ NJTKLF WPCAS UXJLB. - EWCL
XALLWL

459.

YR KBUKSQ QLLOQ YOCGQQYEBL NHRYB

YR'Q JGHL. - HLBQGH OKHJLBK

. . . .

460.

JVXK VN P LPHVQE PLRKQAMHK CH

QCABVQE PA PJJ. - BKJKQ FKJJKH

. . . .

461.

SYZGFSL FH XYYWBA JSI VYAB JZZAJXZFCB

ZGJS J QFL XYVBQJXP, JSI ZGJZ'WW QB VB.

- HZBCBS JIWBA

. . . .

462.

MTD ZDSVM RQ FUU MTVILJ UVDJ VI MTDVS

PVQQVEYUMC. - FUDNFIPSD PYZFJ

. . . .

463.

DK DE XRK YXRLSB KR HDA, TRL ALEK BDK.

- DKHIDHX VORJYOZ

. . . .

464.

UFJR ADOOAF DZ EFFVFV OL CBNF B

MBTTR ADPF. DO DZ BAA HDOMDE

RLQJZFAP, DE RLQJ HBR LP OMDENDEI. -

CBJWQZ BQJFADQZ

. . . .

465.

UDABVILMI WE UDABWDM S FAJSFA WE S

YQCWF. BWELAJ WE DAF TCFFWDM WF WD

S YQCWF ESVSL. - JWVIE UWDMFAD

. . . .

466.

OKJA KY DHKB. HBTCBA UPC YHTY CFPAIUKYA KY YAOOKBZ YCGAFPKBZ. - UKOOKHG ZCOQGHB

. . . .

467.

G VCXCZ JZCHUCJ HDWSA NSMMCNN, G QWZECJ YWZ GA. - CNACC BHSJCZ

. . . .

468.

ZHV OVMG CD GPD YPKQFD ZHV REMP GH MDD EQ GPD RHJWS. - OKPKGOK FKQSPE

. . . .

469.

MC TRK JNDZ ZR XRRV ZSMD, SNDI RKZ JMZS CNZ QARQXA. - BRODAT ONDIABCMAXO

. . . .

470.

FLC XGK'H OTZTKO LK FLCV TFTQ YETK FLCV RNGMRKGHRLK RQ LCH LP PLXCQ. - NGVA HYGRK

. . . .

471.

UWI SBG GDQ OUDR ZBKEJV, EO UWI SBG GDQ XEJ UWI ZBKI. - FDF HBZMIG

. . . .

472.

YVK YKBEYUYWDM DZ YVK UXK WJ YD

TDDR XDDP LWYVDGY OKWMX XDDP. -

OIKMMUM BUMMWMX

. . . .

473.

SBXE PZNU MYTZ RYMM GBU PZ TBXGL YG

OBCTBEU. YU RYMM PZ TBXGL YG

TYHVUYGH TBE RVFU SBX PZMYZKZ YG. -

CFJYCZ MFHFOZ

. . . .

474.

TK UGQKLMTOK. CL UCYGAMYK

WCSLQKON. HJMYKAKL JMQ YC TK PCDK,

GY'Q MOHMWQ WCSL ZJCGZK. - HMWDK

PWKL

475.

VQXPX OPX ZOP, ZOP YXVVXP VQLHSM OQXON VQOH OHW UX AXODX YXQLHN. - E.M. AXULM

476.

NTWWTX WU RAT VWEKRAKB WFEK WU QAGT UK HUOX MKTTV. - TXKTVWU

477.

DPN CBQJ IPMEP PFC HB WMONT SQGSBCN MH JMWN MC JBCD. DB UN NXNGLIPNGN, MC DB UN HBIPNGN. - VMEPNJ TN VBHDFMZHN

478.

LQ NGM IXWE NGMB YSLRPBFW EG RLOEFW, EBN EXRTLWD OGQERN EG OGCFGWF FROF. - XWW RXWPFBO

. . . .

479.

YP SAAPFCUXIR WKNSY YRXGWI, QN FLIY GPY PGUH SAY, JLY SUIP EKNSF, GPY PGUH CUSG, JLY SUIP JNUXNMN. - SGSYPUN TKSGAN

. . . .

480.

OJ YKRRLA DQKR ZJW'AL XJUOX RQAJWXQ, RQLAL'P K CUXQR KR RQL LOB JG RQL RWOOLC. - BLYU CJSKRJ

. . . .

481.

OH ON YIH OY HWL NHVUN HI WIEK IDU
KLNHOYR GDH OY IDUNLEJLN. - FOEEOVP
NWVBLNZLVUL

. . . .

482.

PZLXPWBUPMZ RMSDL QWMS KPUOPZ
HMCWLDVQ. MZD OBL UM ID XMLPUPJD.
KODZ HMC'WD XMLPUPJD, NMMY UOPZNL
OBXXDZ. - YDDX WMH

. . . .

483.

E NVFMR BNMMFS BONMIR SOR ZFDVX,
PGS E BNM BNKS N KSFMR NBDFKK SOR
ZNSRD SF BDRNSR UNMJ DEYYVRK. -
UFSORD SRDRKN

484.

GPB FPJ'M FSPEJ HG DXRRTJL TJ EXMYS.
GPB FSPEJ HG OMXGTJL MQYSY. - SPHYSM
IPRRTYS

485.

RJM ZOHP BMLDZO PZG DJZGHY RLP RZ QM
QMRRML RJCO, SD RJM BMLDZO PZG TMLM
PMDRMLYCP. - VCRRP VGHHMOD

486.

VJYD MNNRM DB CM YM HWDDNQ DQWYZM
YQN BSDNX HZNMMWXOM WX IWMOCWMN.
- BMUYQ VWZIN

165

487.

CUFO BQXO ZIQX PIXBW OLOCZ NIOBL'W

VDTO GOWPOOL ZIQX IPL WPI OUXB. -

VUDXN EUCDVWIL

. . . .

488.

WCKJE IX HWS CUS WCKJE IX KNPW BCTWP

C BCU RWCJIRE, FWCJIRE, CUS FNPW. -

HWUVCBNU DKCUTJNU

. . . .

489.

OJX SRLL 100 NVAZVIM JY MCV LCJML OJX

IVFVA MWQV. - TWOIV UAVMGQO

. . . .

490.

SVDD XV YER Q KUJTVS. SVYWG XV YER Q
JVXVXHVJ. QEBUDBV XV YER Q DVYJE. -
HVEMYXQE KJYEZDQE

. . . .

491.

DH EW YWN GHAHARHG ESJP, DH
GHAHARHG AWAHYNP. - IHPSGH FSMHPH

. . . .

492.

NSBT SOQ'P WZYDP BSQXSQA UYDGOTNB.
NSBT SO WZYDP VGTWPSQA UYDGOTNB. -
ATYGAT ZTGQWGX OFWM

. . . .

493.

QWQU DBQ OHUQYD YCZIA XJKUTQA HUDZ
YPJD CPDQI CHJJ QWQUDKPJJR IKYD. - YKU
DNK

. . . .

494.

BJKKZANVV ZV AEU HG XBJAXN, HTU HG
XBEZXN. - YZF PEBA

. . . .

495.

WVVK UXDZ VUVR XL EBV REHZR, HLG
UXDZ MVVE XL EBV CZXDLG. - EBVXGXZV
ZXXRVTVPE

. . . .

496.

NPSXRZ   HTME   KPTMRPKG   SXL   HTM
NPSXRZ HTME QTEUL. - XTEDSX

497.

A SAEN ZKUZ ZKT KUJNTJ A RCJL, ZKT WCJT VBOL A DTTW ZC KUFT. - ZKCWUD MTSSTJDCE

. . . .

498.

N SNR CLLC JR PKL ZFBXT ZKNP KL UNBBJLC JR KJC KLNBP. - IFKNRR ZFXHWNRW QFR WFLPKL

. . . .

499.

XT QYRBMEGD XYHOEKD YG GOD STX EJ GOD RDKNEKS XYHOEKD. - HYMBPEKD MODY

. . . .

500.

JARNMBR MFVPF SMRNASH OWS PUAQR,

JARNMBR ONWMQ SMRNASH OWS PDMZDP.

- WSMS

. . . .

HINTS

1: R=I	2: V=O	3: Y=T
4: Q=I	5: D=T	6: U=T
7: Q=I	8: U=O	9: M=S
10: P=E	11: D=O	12: K=O
13: R=E	14: F=A	15: R=O
16: D=H	17: H=T	18: T=A
19: Y=E	20: W=A	21: T=E
22: N=A	23: E=A	24: X=N
25: O=T	26: B=I	27: H=A
28: U=E	29: M=E	30: F=E
31: U=E	32: K=I	33: L=T
34: N=T	35: Q=N	36: C=E
37: U=O	38: M=I	39: Z=I
40: U=T	41: O=A	42: X=I
43: K=N	44: N=T	45: P=E
46: O=A	47: O=I	48: F=E

49: L=E	50: J=N	51: R=I
52: M=E	53: O=N	54: F=S
55: E=A	56: A=O	57: U=O
58: X=T	59: S=E	60: U=S
61: Q=E	62: I=R	63: T=I
64: P=N	65: K=R	66: J=T
67: O=T	68: C=A	69: F=A
70: M=N	71: K=A	72: J=A
73: F=E	74: W=A	75: U=R
76: O=E	77: E=I	78: N=O
79: Q=N	80: Q=N	81: F=O
82: A=O	83: U=O	84: A=I
85: Y=E	86: C=A	87: M=R
88: V=E	89: H=E	90: Q=R
91: Q=N	92: K=T	93: J=O
94: C=O	95: Z=E	96: C=R

97: N=T	98: E=I	99: P=N
100: I=S	101: M=I	102: L=A
103: L=A	104: S=O	105: Q=R
106: D=O	107: P=T	108: A=O
109: E=O	110: Y=I	111: R=E
112: L=E	113: R=O	114: Z=I
115: X=E	116: O=T	117: Y=I
118: Z=O	119: Y=S	120: A=I
121: G=T	122: R=A	123: W=I
124: K=T	125: K=E	126: D=E
127: B=E	128: G=E	129: L=D
130: V=A	131: O=A	132: H=E
133: O=E	134: I=R	135: G=E
136: L=T	137: Z=E	138: H=E
139: F=E	140: G=O	141: O=H
142: N=I	143: O=E	144: H=D

145: G=A	146: O=A	147: F=E
148: J=O	149: G=N	150: X=I
151: I=E	152: E=O	153: F=E
154: E=N	155: F=O	156: F=A
157: M=O	158: V=N	159: G=H
160: Y=T	161: R=T	162: Y=E
163: F=N	164: W=O	165: U=I
166: R=E	167: H=T	168: Q=S
169: G=A	170: P=M	171: N=T
172: X=H	173: G=O	174: D=A
175: P=R	176: Q=T	177: N=E
178: E=O	179: X=A	180: B=O
181: R=A	182: H=N	183: U=T
184: F=I	185: V=A	186: C=E
187: U=A	188: K=I	189: V=O
190: F=R	191: V=O	192: Z=I

193: T=E	194: M=I	195: H=A
196: Q=R	197: T=E	198: K=O
199: I=E	200: M=E	201: L=T
202: D=T	203: L=S	204: H=N
205: M=R	206: O=I	207: J=E
208: H=T	209: D=O	210: I=O
211: M=T	212: Q=O	213: D=E
214: B=N	215: S=T	216: R=N
217: I=E	218: O=T	219: A=E
220: V=I	221: X=R	222: D=I
223: A=W	224: R=I	225: I=O
226: N=A	227: C=T	228: I=A
229: F=N	230: F=I	231: H=O
232: E=S	233: R=O	234: D=E
235: L=E	236: M=E	237: M=I
238: G=E	239: P=R	240: I=O

241: W=S	242: G=A	243: K=O
244: H=O	245: E=T	246: W=E
247: U=N	248: G=R	249: G=E
250: P=T	251: P=A	252: M=A
253: J=T	254: B=O	255: M=T
256: W=T	257: Z=O	258: M=S
259: J=N	260: Q=A	261: F=A
262: R=N	263: O=E	264: G=A
265: U=N	266: C=O	267: P=I
268: N=A	269: K=A	270: K=T
271: K=E	272: X=O	273: A=E
274: T=E	275: J=T	276: O=E
277: H=A	278: I=T	279: H=I
280: K=E	281: Y=H	282: S=E
283: M=R	284: A=H	285: L=A
286: R=A	287: K=E	288: K=A

289: S=A	290: T=O	291: Q=N
292: L=A	293: Y=O	294: Z=O
295: S=A	296: E=I	297: B=E
298: C=E	299: D=I	300: I=O
301: N=E	302: V=I	303: C=T
304: A=O	305: Z=M	306: Z=A
307: W=E	308: F=I	309: H=T
310: U=R	311: L=I	312: O=H
313: R=I	314: P=E	315: O=R
316: E=R	317: J=O	318: T=O
319: O=A	320: F=I	321: O=E
322: Y=A	323: D=N	324: J=E
325: J=I	326: M=O	327: V=M
328: V=O	329: C=A	330: U=N
331: D=T	332: S=H	333: M=N
334: L=O	335: Y=E	336: F=M

337: M=E	338: Z=A	339: L=T
340: G=E	341: Q=O	342: K=O
343: R=T	344: R=N	345: G=A
346: I=N	347: A=E	348: E=I
349: X=N	350: I=A	351: L=I
352: N=I	353: P=N	354: B=I
355: T=E	356: U=T	357: T=O
358: K=T	359: F=O	360: Z=O
361: X=S	362: D=E	363: P=E
364: W=T	365: T=A	366: A=O
367: P=N	368: K=N	369: B=S
370: T=N	371: R=N	372: Q=O
373: M=E	374: V=E	375: N=T
376: O=A	377: Q=O	378: J=T
379: O=T	380: M=I	381: X=O
382: S=I	383: N=A	384: G=A

385: E=A	386: P=A	387: M=S
388: T=O	389: F=R	390: V=S
391: H=E	392: Y=T	393: D=O
394: S=T	395: O=S	396: T=E
397: N=E	398: R=A	399: N=S
400: V=E	401: Y=I	402: M=T
403: D=E	404: N=E	405: C=I
406: I=S	407: F=A	408: S=H
409: G=E	410: W=E	411: K=O
412: S=E	413: R=N	414: T=O
415: P=A	416: P=S	417: H=E
418: P=O	419: V=H	420: X=N
421: A=O	422: G=A	423: X=T
424: K=E	425: H=T	426: G=R
427: C=A	428: Z=A	429: S=R
430: B=I	431: B=I	432: E=I

433: S=O	434: Y=E	435: H=E
436: R=E	437: T=E	438: F=R
439: G=T	440: J=E	441: X=E
442: B=T	443: V=O	444: I=E
445: R=E	446: F=S	447: V=E
448: N=I	449: X=I	450: M=N
451: P=E	452: Y=E	453: J=E
454: F=E	455: G=I	456: Y=A
457: B=T	458: A=E	459: L=E
460: P=A	461: B=E	462: D=E
463: K=T	464: F=E	465: F=T
466: Y=S	467: Z=R	468: P=H
469: Z=T	470: K=N	471: I=E
472: M=N	473: Z=E	474: M=A
475: O=A	476: W=T	477: M=I
478: F=E	479: Y=T	480: L=E

481: L=E	482: D=E	483: N=A
484: S=R	485: R=T	486: N=E
487: I=O	488: W=E	489: M=T
490: E=N	491: A=M	492: S=I
493: D=T	494: Z=I	495: X=O
496: X=N	497: K=H	498: N=A
499: Y=A	500: M=O	

SOLUTIONS

1.

THE MOST COMMON WAY PEOPLE GIVE UP THEIR POWER IS

BY THINKING THEY DON'T HAVE ANY. - ALICE WALKER

2.

THE SECRET OF SUCCESS IS TO DO THE COMMON THING

UNCOMMONLY WELL. - JOHN D. ROCKEFELLER JR.

3.

THE MOST WASTED OF DAYS IS ONE WITHOUT LAUGHTER. -

E. E. CUMMINGS

4.

I CAN'T CHANGE THE DIRECTION OF THE WIND, BUT I CAN

ADJUST MY SAILS TO ALWAYS REACH MY DESTINATION. -

JIMMY DEAN

5.

EVERY TIME SOMETHING POPS IN MY HEAD, I THINK TWICE

ABOUT IT AND I DO IT ANYWAY. - GILBERT GOTTFRIED

6.

WHEN YOU'VE GOT SOMETHING TO PROVE, THERE'S NOTHING GREATER THAN A CHALLENGE. - TERRY BRADSHAW

7.

WHEN I LET GO OF WHAT I AM, I BECOME WHAT I MIGHT BE. - LAO TZU

8.

MY BEST BIRTH CONTROL NOW IS JUST TO LEAVE THE LIGHTS ON. - JOAN RIVERS

9.

IT IS DURING OUR DARKEST MOMENTS THAT WE MUST FOCUS TO SEE THE LIGHT. - ARISTOTLE ONASSIS

10.

WHEN YOU REACH THE END OF YOUR ROPE, TIE A KNOT IN IT AND HANG ON. - FRANKLIN D. ROOSEVELT

11.

EDUCATION IS THE MOST POWERFUL WEAPON WHICH YOU CAN USE TO CHANGE THE WORLD. - NELSON MANDELA

12.

WINE IS CONSTANT PROOF THAT GOD LOVES US AND LOVES TO SEE US HAPPY. - BENJAMIN FRANKLIN

13.

TO BE SURE OF HITTING THE TARGET, SHOOT FIRST, AND CALL WHATEVER YOU HIT THE TARGET. - ASHLEIGH BRILLIANT

14.

REAL DIFFICULTIES CAN BE OVERCOME. IT IS ONLY THE IMAGINARY ONES THAT ARE UNCONQUERABLE. - THEODORE N. VAIL

15.

PRESS FORWARD. DO NOT STOP, DO NOT LINGER IN YOUR JOURNEY, BUT STRIVE FOR THE MARK SET BEFORE YOU. - GEORGE WHITEFIELD

16.

THINK BIG THOUGHTS BUT RELISH SMALL PLEASURES. - JACKSON BROWN JR.

17.

HE WHO IS UNTRUE TO HIS OWN CAUSE CANNOT COMMAND THE RESPECT OF OTHERS. - ALBERT EINSTEIN

18.

IT'S NOT WHAT YOU LOOK AT THAT MATTERS, IT'S WHAT YOU SEE. - HENRY DAVID THOREAU

19.

IF YOU ARE LIVING OUT OF A SENSE OF OBLIGATION YOU ARE A SLAVE. - DR. WAYNE DYER

20.

YOU MAY HAVE TO FIGHT A BATTLE MORE THAN ONCE TO WIN IT. - MARGARET THATCHER

21.

LOOK FOR THE THING YOU NOTICE BUT NO ONE ELSE NOTICES. - RICK RUBIN

22.

CHALLENGES ARE WHAT MAKE LIFE INTERESTING. OVERCOMING THEM IS WHAT MAKES LIFE MEANINGFUL. - JOSHUA MARINE

23.

LIFE DOES NOT OWE YOU ANYTHING BECAUSE LIFE HAS ALREADY GIVEN YOU EVERYTHING. - RALPH MARSTON

24.

WHEN EVERYTHING IS COMING YOUR WAY, YOU'RE IN THE WRONG LANE. - STEVEN WRIGHT

25.

BETTER TO LIGHT A CANDLE THAN TO CURSE THE DARKNESS. - CHINESE PROVERB

26.

WE NO LONGER LIVE LIFE. WE CONSUME IT. - VICKI ROBIN

27.

PERFECTION IS NOT ATTAINABLE, BUT IF WE CHASE PERFECTION WE CAN CATCH EXCELLENCE. - VINCE LOMBARDI

28.

ONCE YOU SAY YOU'RE GOING TO SETTLE FOR SECOND, THAT'S WHAT HAPPENS TO YOU IN LIFE. - JOHN F. KENNEDY

29.

MY MISSION IN LIFE IS NOT MERELY TO SURVIVE, BUT TO THRIVE. - MAYA ANGELOU

30.

SUCCESS USUALLY COMES TO THOSE WHO ARE TOO BUSY TO BE LOOKING FOR IT. - HENRY DAVID THOREAU

31.

AN OBSTACLE IS OFTEN A STEPPING STONE. - PRESCOTT

32.

BELIEVE THAT LIFE IS WORTH LIVING AND YOUR BELIEF WILL HELP CREATE THE FACT. - WILLIAM JAMES

33.

WE ARE WHAT WE REPEATEDLY DO. EXCELLENCE, THEN, IS NOT AN ACT, BUT A HABIT. - ARISTOTLE

34.

EVERYTHING HAS BEAUTY, BUT NOT EVERYONE SEES IT. - CONFUCIUS

35.

KNOWING TREES, I UNDERSTAND THE MEANING OF PATIENCE. KNOWING GRASS, I CAN APPRECIATE PERSISTENCE. - HAL BORLAND

36.

IF MY LIFE IS GOING TO MEAN ANYTHING, I HAVE TO LIVE IT MYSELF. - RICK RIORDAN

37.

PEOPLE ARE MORE IMPRESSED BY THE POWER OF OUR EXAMPLE RATHER THAN THE EXAMPLE OF OUR POWER. - BILL CLINTON

38.

NURTURE YOUR MIND WITH GREAT THOUGHTS. TO BELIEVE IN THE HEROIC MAKES HEROES. - BENJAMIN DISRAELI

39.

LIFE IS NOT ABOUT HOW FAST YOU RUN OR HOW HIGH YOU CLIMB, BUT HOW WELL YOU BOUNCE. - VIVIAN KOMORI

40.

STRIVE NOT TO BE A SUCCESS, BUT RATHER TO BE OF VALUE. - ALBERT EINSTEIN

41.

IT IS BETTER TO HAVE A MEANINGFUL LIFE AND MAKE A DIFFERENCE THAN TO MERELY HAVE A LONG LIFE. - BRYANT H. MCGILL

42.

I AM ONLY HUMAN, ALTHOUGH I REGRET IT. - MARK TWAIN

43.

THERE IS ONLY ONE MOTIVATION, AND THAT IS DESIRE. NO REASONS OR PRINCIPLE CONTAIN IT OR STAND AGAINST IT. - JANE SMILEY

44.

THERE IS NOTHING SO USELESS AS DOING EFFICIENTLY THAT WHICH SHOULD NOT BE DONE AT ALL. - PETER DRUCKER

45.

TOGETHER WE CAN FACE ANY CHALLENGES AS DEEP AS THE OCEAN AND AS HIGH AS THE SKY. - SONIA GANDHI

46.

YOU'VE GOTTA DANCE LIKE THERE'S NOBODY WATCHING. - WILLIAM W. PURKEY

47.

EVERYTHING YOU CAN IMAGINE IS REAL. - PABLO PICASSO

48.

SOME PEOPLE LOOK FOR A BEAUTIFUL PLACE. OTHERS MAKE A PLACE BEAUTIFUL. - HAZRAT INAYAT KHAN

49.

BETTER TO DO SOMETHING IMPERFECTLY THAN TO DO NOTHING FLAWLESSLY. - ROBERT SCHULLER

50.

THE BEST THINGS IN LIFE ARE FREE. THE SECOND BEST THINGS ARE VERY EXPENSIVE. - COCO CHANEL

51.

SUCCESS IS NOT FINAL, FAILURE IS NOT FATAL. IT IS THE COURAGE TO CONTINUE THAT COUNTS. - WINSTON CHURCHILL

52.

I HAVE NO SPECIAL TALENT. I AM ONLY PASSIONATELY CURIOUS. - ALBERT EINSTEIN

53.

HAPPINESS OFTEN SNEAKS IN THROUGH A DOOR YOU DIDN'T KNOW YOU LEFT OPEN. - JOHN BARRYMORE

54.

DEATH IS NOT THE GREATEST LOSS IN LIFE. THE GREATEST LOSS IS WHAT DIES INSIDE US WHILE WE LIVE. - NORMAN COUSINS

55.

I HAVE LEARNED OVER THE YEARS THAT WHEN ONE'S MIND IS MADE UP, THIS DIMINISHES FEAR. - ROSA PARKS

56.

IF YOU CONTINUE TO THINK THE WAY YOU'VE ALWAYS THOUGHT, YOU'LL CONTINUE TO GET WHAT YOU'VE ALWAYS GOT. - KEVIN TRUDEAU

57.

WHEN WE STRIVE TO BECOME BETTER THAN WE ARE, EVERYTHING AROUND US BECOMES BETTER TOO. - PAULO COELHO

58.

IT IS BETTER TO FAIL IN ORIGINALITY THAN TO SUCCEED IN IMITATION. - HERMAN MELVILLE

59.

LET US MAKE OUR FUTURE NOW, AND LET US MAKE OUR DREAMS TOMORROW'S REALITY. - MALALA YOUSAFZAI

60.

THE FULLNESS OF LIFE IS ONLY ACCESSIBLE IN THE PRESENT

MOMENT. - ECKHART TOLLE

61.

IF YOU WANT TO LIVE A HAPPY LIFE, TIE IT TO A GOAL, NOT

TO PEOPLE OR THINGS. - ALBERT EINSTEIN

62.

YESTERDAY IS NOT OURS TO RECOVER, BUT TOMORROW IS

OURS TO WIN OR LOSE. - LYNDON JOHNSON

63.

I ALWAYS WANTED TO BE SOMEBODY, BUT NOW I REALIZE I

SHOULD HAVE BEEN MORE SPECIFIC. - LILY TOMLIN

64.

WE SUFFER MORE OFTEN IN IMAGINATION THAN IN REALITY.

- SENECA

65.

IT IS EASIER TO BUILD STRONG CHILDREN THAN TO REPAIR BROKEN MEN. - FREDERICK DOUGLASS

66.

DON'T USE YESTERDAY'S STATE OF MIND, TO MAKE TODAY'S DECISION. - C. NZINGHA SMITH

67.

LIFE IS TEN PERCENT WHAT HAPPENS TO YOU AND NINETY PERCENT HOW YOU RESPOND TO IT. - LOU HOLTZ

68.

YOU ARE ONLY AS FREE AS YOU THINK YOU ARE AND FREEDOM WILL ALWAYS BE AS REAL AS YOU BELIEVE IT TO BE. - ROBERT M. DRAKE

69.

ALL MEN WHO HAVE ACHIEVED GREAT THINGS HAVE BEEN GREAT DREAMERS. - ORISON SWETT MARDEN

70.

I TAKE MY WIFE EVERYWHERE, BUT SHE KEEPS FINDING HER WAY BACK. - HENNY YOUNGMAN

71.

EVERYTHING THAT IRRITATES US ABOUT OTHERS CAN LEAD US TO AN UNDERSTANDING OF OURSELVES. - CARL JUNG

72.

THOSE WHO DARE TO FAIL MISERABLY CAN ACHIEVE GREATLY. - JOHN F. KENNEDY

73.

OUR GREATEST FEAR SHOULD NOT BE OF FAILURE BUT OF SUCCEEDING AT THINGS IN LIFE THAT DON'T REALLY MATTER. - FRANCIS CHAN

74.

BE THE CHANGE THAT YOU WISH TO SEE IN THE WORLD. - MAHATMA GANDHI

75.

YOU MAY FIND THE WORST ENEMY OR BEST FRIEND IN YOURSELF. - ENGLISH PROVERB

76.

WE ARE EVOLVED TO SEARCH FOR MEANING BUT ULTIMATELY LIFE HAS NONE. - NAVAL RAVIKANT

77.

THE UNEXAMINED LIFE IS NOT WORTH LIVING. - SOCRATES

78.

DON'T BE PUSHED BY YOUR PROBLEMS, BE LED BY YOUR DREAMS. - RALPH WALDO EMERSON

79.

THAT'S ONE SMALL STEP FOR A MAN, ONE GIANT LEAP FOR MANKIND. - NEIL ARMSTRONG

80.

HAPPINESS IS HAVING A LARGE, LOVING, CARING, CLOSE KNIT FAMILY IN ANOTHER CITY. - GEORGE BURNS

81.

IF YOU JUDGE PEOPLE, YOU HAVE NO TIME TO LOVE THEM. - MOTHER TERESA

82.

THE ROAD TO SUCCESS IS ALWAYS UNDER CONSTRUCTION. - LILY TOMLIN

83.

AS WE LOOK AHEAD INTO THE NEXT CENTURY, LEADERS WILL BE THOSE WHO EMPOWER OTHERS. - BILL GATES

84.

AGE IS AN ISSUE OF MIND OVER MATTER. IF YOU DON'T MIND, IT DOESN'T MATTER. - MARK TWAIN

85.

WOMEN CANNOT COMPLAIN ABOUT MEN ANYMORE UNTIL THEY START GETTING BETTER TASTE IN THEM. - BILL MAHER

86.

IT ISN'T THE MOUNTAINS AHEAD TO CLIMB THAT WEAR YOU OUT, IT'S THE PEBBLE IN YOUR SHOE. - MUHAMMAD ALI

87.

YOU CAN TELL A PIONEER BY THE ARROWS IN HIS BACK. - BEVERLY RUBIK

88.

LIFE IS LIKE A BOX OF CHOCOLATES. YOU NEVER KNOW WHAT YOU'RE GOING TO GET. - FORREST GUMP

89.

THE SMALLEST ACT OF KINDNESS IS WORTH MORE THAN THE GREATEST INTENTION. - KAHLIL GIBRAN

90.

IN THREE WORDS I CAN SUM UP EVERYTHING I'VE LEARNED ABOUT LIFE. IT GOES ON. - ROBERT FROST

91.

TRUTH IS EVER TO BE FOUND IN SIMPLICITY, AND NOT IN THE MULTIPLICITY AND CONFUSION OF THINGS. - ISAAC NEWTON

92.

ALL THAT WE ARE IS THE RESULT OF WHAT WE HAVE THOUGHT. - BUDDHA

93.

A PESSIMIST IS A PERSON WHO HAS HAD TO LISTEN TO TOO MANY OPTIMISTS. - DON MARQUIS

94.

LUCK IS A DIVIDEND OF SWEAT. THE MORE YOU SWEAT, THE LUCKIER YOU GET. - RAY KROC

95.

IF YOU THINK YOU ARE TOO SMALL TO MAKE A DIFFERENCE,
TRY SLEEPING WITH A MOSQUITO. - DALAI LAMA

96.

ORIGINALITY IS THE FINE ART OF REMEMBERING WHAT YOU
HEAR BUT FORGETTING WHERE YOU HEARD IT. - LAURENCE
J. PETER

97.

THE ONLY LIMIT TO OUR REALIZATION OF TOMORROW WILL
BE OUR DOUBTS OF TODAY. - FRANKLIN D. ROOSEVELT

98.

MOTIVATION IS WHAT GETS YOU STARTED. HABIT IS WHAT
KEEPS YOU GOING. - JIM ROHN

99.

A THOUSAND WORDS WILL NOT LEAVE SO DEEP AN
IMPRESSION AS ONE DEED. - HENRIK IBSEN

100.

THAT WHICH DOES NOT KILL US MAKES US STRONGER. - FRIEDRICH NIETZSCHE

101.

IF YOU'RE GOING THROUGH HELL, KEEP GOING. - WINSTON CHURCHILL

102.

MARRIAGE IS THE ONLY WAR IN WHICH YOU SLEEP WITH THE ENEMY. - FRANCOIS DE LA ROCHEFOUCAULD

103.

WHEN YOU HAVE A DREAM, YOU'VE GOT TO GRAB IT AND NEVER LET GO. - CAROL BURNETT

104.

NEVER GO TO A DOCTOR WHOSE OFFICE PLANTS HAVE DIED. - ERMA BOMBECK

105.

EVEN IF YOU'RE ON THE RIGHT TRACK, YOU'LL GET RUN OVER IF YOU JUST SIT THERE. - WILL ROGERS

106.

HAVE YOU NOTICED THAT ALL THE PEOPLE IN FAVOR OF BIRTH CONTROL ARE ALREADY BORN? - BENNY HILL

107.

EVEN IF I KNEW THAT TOMORROW THE WORLD WOULD GO TO PIECES, I WOULD STILL PLANT MY APPLE TREE. - MARTIN LUTHER

108.

THE ONLY PERSON YOU ARE DESTINED TO BECOME IS THE PERSON YOU DECIDE TO BE. - RALPH WALDO EMERSON

109.

SPREAD LOVE EVERYWHERE YOU GO. LET NO ONE EVER COME TO YOU WITHOUT LEAVING HAPPIER. - MOTHER TERESA

110.

MANY RECEIVE ADVICE, ONLY THE WISE PROFIT FROM IT. - HARPER LEE

111.

DON'T BE AFRAID TO GIVE UP THE GOOD TO GO FOR THE GREAT. - JOHN D. ROCKEFELLER

112.

PERPETUAL OPTIMISM IS A FORCE MULTIPLIER. - COLIN POWELL

113.

FOR EVERY MINUTE YOU ARE ANGRY YOU LOSE 60 SECONDS OF HAPPINESS. - RALPH WALDO EMERSON

114.

I'M SICK OF FOLLOWING MY DREAMS. I'M JUST GOING TO ASK WHERE THEY'RE GOING AND HOOK UP WITH THEM LATER. - MITCH HEDBERG

115.

MISTAKES ARE PART OF THE DUES THAT ONE PAYS FOR A FULL LIFE. - SOPHIA LOREN

116.

GOOD THINGS COME TO PEOPLE WHO WAIT, BUT BETTER THINGS COME TO THOSE WHO GO OUT AND GET THEM. - ANONYMOUS

117.

I AM THANKFUL FOR ALL OF THOSE WHO SAID NO TO ME. IT'S BECAUSE OF THEM I'M DOING IT MYSELF. - ALBERT EINSTEIN

118.

STAY HUNGRY, STAY FOOLISH. - STEVE JOBS

119.

DON'T KEEP A MAN GUESSING TOO LONG. HE'S SURE TO FIND THE ANSWER SOMEWHERE ELSE. - MAE WEST

120.

NOTHING IS IMPOSSIBLE. THE WORD ITSELF SAYS I'M POSSIBLE. - AUDREY HEPBURN

121.

ALL YOU NEED IS LOVE. BUT A LITTLE CHOCOLATE NOW AND THEN DOESN'T HURT. - CHARLES SCHULZ

122.

YOU DO NOT FIND THE HAPPY LIFE. YOU MAKE IT. - CAMILLA EYRING KIMBALL

123.

DON'T CRY BECAUSE IT'S OVER, SMILE BECAUSE IT HAPPENED. - LUDWIG JACOBOWSKI

124.

I WANT TO BE LIKE WATER. I WANT TO SLIP THROUGH FINGERS, BUT HOLD UP A SHIP. - MICHELLE WILLIAMS

125.

GENIUS IS ONE PERCENT INSPIRATION, NINETY-NINE PERCENT PERSPIRATION. - THOMAS A. EDISON

126.

THERE ARE BETTER STARTERS THAN ME, BUT I'M A STRONG FINISHER. - USAIN BOLT

127.

THE SAFE WAY TO DOUBLE YOUR MONEY IS TO FOLD IT OVER ONCE AND PUT IT IN YOUR POCKET. - KIN HUBBARD

128.

YOU MUST NOT LET ANYONE DEFINE YOUR LIMITS BECAUSE OF WHERE YOU COME FROM. YOUR ONLY LIMIT IS YOUR SOUL. - WALT DISNEY

129.

DO OR DO NOT. THERE IS NO TRY. - YODA

130.

THE SECRET OF A HAPPY MARRIAGE REMAINS A SECRET. - HENNY YOUNGMAN

131.

WISE MEN TALK BECAUSE THEY HAVE SOMETHING TO SAY. FOOLS, BECAUSE THEY HAVE TO SAY SOMETHING. - PLATO

132.

THE PATH TO SUCCESS IS TO TAKE MASSIVE, DETERMINED ACTION. - TONY ROBBINS

133.

BUILD YOUR OWN DREAMS, OR SOMEONE ELSE WILL HIRE YOU TO BUILD THEIRS. - FARRAH GRAY

134.

LIFE CAN ONLY BE UNDERSTOOD BACKWARDS BUT IT MUST BE LIVED FORWARDS. - SOREN KIERKEGAARD

135.

LIFE IS FROM THE INSIDE OUT. WHEN YOU SHIFT ON THE INSIDE, LIFE SHIFTS ON THE OUTSIDE. - KAMAL RAVIKANT

136.

THE HARDER THE BATTLE, THE SWEETER THE VICTORY. - LES BROWN

137.

THE BEST WAY TO PREDICT THE FUTURE IS TO CREATE IT. - ABRAHAM LINCOLN

138.

IF YOU HAVE EVERYTHING UNDER CONTROL, YOU'RE NOT MOVING FAST ENOUGH. - MARIO ANDRETTI

139.

JUST WHEN THE CATERPILLAR THOUGHT THE WORLD WAS ENDING, HE TURNED INTO A BUTTERFLY. - PROVERB

140.

IF YOU REALIZED HOW POWERFUL YOUR THOUGHTS ARE, YOU WOULD NEVER THINK A NEGATIVE THOUGHT. - PEACE PILGRIM

141.

WE CAN SEE THROUGH OTHERS ONLY WHEN WE CAN SEE THROUGH OURSELVES. - BRUCE LEE

142.

I WANT MY CHILDREN TO HAVE ALL THE THINGS I COULDN'T AFFORD. THEN I WANT TO MOVE IN WITH THEM. - PHYLLIS DILLER

143.

ALWAYS MAKE A TOTAL EFFORT, EVEN WHEN THE ODDS ARE AGAINST YOU. - ARNOLD PALMER

144.

THE GOOD LIFE IS INSPIRED BY LOVE AND GUIDED BY KNOWLEDGE. - BERTRAND RUSSELL

145.

LIFE IS NOT MEASURED BY THE NUMBER OF BREATHS WE TAKE, BUT BY THE MOMENTS THAT TAKE OUR BREATH AWAY. - MAYA ANGELOU

146.

THERE ARE TWO GREAT DAYS IN A PERSON'S LIFE. THE DAY WE ARE BORN AND THE DAY WE DISCOVER WHY. - WILLIAM BARCLAY

147.

SPEAK LESS THAN YOU KNOW, HAVE MORE THAN YOU SHOW. - WILLIAM SHAKESPEARE

148.

WHAT GREAT THING WOULD YOU ATTEMPT IF YOU KNEW YOU COULD NOT FAIL? - ROBERT H. SCHULLER

149.

FORGIVE YOUR ENEMIES, BUT NEVER FORGET THEIR NAMES. - JOHN F. KENENDY

150.

LIFE IS BEING ON THE WIRE, EVERYTHING ELSE IS JUST WAITING. - KARL WALLENDA

151.

IT'S NOT HOW MUCH YOU HAVE THAT MAKES PEOPLE LOOK UP TO YOU, IT'S WHO YOU ARE. - ELVIS PRESLEY

152.

ALWAYS BORROW MONEY FROM A PESSIMIST. HE WON'T EXPECT IT BACK. - OSCAR WILDE

153.

I LOVE THOSE WHO CAN SMILE IN TROUBLE. - LEONARDO DA VINCI

154.

I HAVE NEVER IN MY LIFE LEARNED ANYTHING FROM ANY MAN WHO AGREED WITH ME. - DUDLEY FIELD MALONE

155.

YOU WILL NOT BE PUNISHED FOR YOUR ANGER, YOU WILL BE PUNISHED BY YOUR ANGER. - BUDDHA

156.

I ALONE CANNOT CHANGE THE WORLD, BUT I CAN CAST A STONE ACROSS THE WATER TO CREATE MANY RIPPLES. - MOTHER TERESA

157.

THOSE WHO REALIZE THEIR FOLLY ARE NOT TRUE FOOLS. - ZHUANGZI

158.

THE DIFFERENCE BETWEEN A STUMBLING BLOCK AND A STEPPING STONE IS HOW HIGH YOU RAISE YOUR FOOT. - BENNY LEWIS

159.

I FIND THAT THE HARDER I WORK, THE MORE LUCK I SEEM TO HAVE. - THOMAS JEFFERSON

160.

THE QUESTION ISN'T WHO IS GOING TO LET ME. IT'S WHO IS GOING TO STOP ME. - AYN RAND

161.

DON'T JUDGE EACH DAY BY THE HARVEST YOU REAP BUT BY THE SEEDS THAT YOU PLANT. - ROBERT LOUIS STEVENSON

162.

PEOPLE WHO THINK THEY KNOW EVERYTHING ARE A GREAT ANNOYANCE TO THOSE OF US WHO DO. - ISAAC ASIMOV

163.

LIFE TAKES ON MEANING WHEN YOU BECOME MOTIVATED, SET GOALS AND CHARGE AFTER THEM IN AN UNSTOPPABLE MANNER. - LES BROWN

164.

DON'T SEARCH FOR THE MEANING OF LIFE. SIMPLY BE PRESENT FOR THE PEOPLE YOU LOVE. - MAXIME LAGACE

165.

GOD GAVE US THE GIFT OF LIFE. IT IS UP TO US TO GIVE OURSELVES THE GIFT OF LIVING WELL. - VOLTAIRE

166.

I'VE FAILED OVER AND OVER AND OVER AGAIN IN MY LIFE AND THAT IS WHY I SUCCEED. - MICHAEL JORDAN

167.

DON'T LET THE FEAR OF LOSING BE GREATER THAN THE EXCITEMENT OF WINNING. - ROBERT KIYOSAKI

168.

EVERY IMPULSE THAT WE STRIVE TO STRANGLE BROODS IN THE MIND AND POISONS US. - OSCAR WILDE

169.

IT'S BETTER TO BE A LION FOR A DAY THAN A SHEEP ALL YOUR LIFE. - ELIZABETH KENNY

170.

AIM FOR THE MOON. IF YOU MISS, YOU MAY HIT A STAR. - W. CLEMENT STONE

171.

NEVER LET THE FEAR OF STRIKING OUT KEEP YOU FROM PLAYING THE GAME. - BABE RUTH

172.

THE MIND IS EVERYTHING. WHAT YOU THINK YOU BECOME. - BUDDHA

173.

THE INDIVIDUAL WHO SAYS IT IS NOT POSSIBLE SHOULD GET OUT OF THE WAY OF THOSE DOING IT. - TRICIA CUNNINGHAM

174.

AN ALCOHOLIC IS SOMEONE YOU DON'T LIKE WHO DRINKS AS MUCH AS YOU DO. - DYLAN THOMAS

175.

EVERYTHING YOU'VE EVER WANTED IS ON THE OTHER SIDE OF FEAR. - GEORGE ADDAIR

176.

LIFE IS 10 PERCENT WHAT HAPPENS TO US AND 90 PERCENT HOW WE REACT TO IT. - DENNIS P. KIMBRO

177.

THE MOST DIFFICULT THING IS THE DECISION TO ACT, THE REST IS MERELY TENACITY. - AMELIA EARHART

178.

GREAT THOUGHTS SPEAK ONLY TO THE THOUGHTFUL MIND, BUT GREAT ACTIONS SPEAK TO ALL MANKIND. - THEODORE ROOSEVELT

179.

ALL OUR DREAMS CAN COME TRUE IF WE HAVE THE COURAGE TO PURSUE THEM. - WALT DISNEY

180.

THERE IS NO AGONY LIKE BEARING AN UNTOLD STORY INSIDE OF YOU. - MAYA ANGELOU

181.

OBSTACLES DON'T HAVE TO STOP YOU. IF YOU RUN INTO A WALL, DON'T TURN AROUND AND GIVE UP. - MICHAEL JORDAN

182.

DON'T LET WHAT YOU CANNOT DO INTERFERE WITH WHAT YOU CAN DO. - JOHN WOODEN

183.

YOU MUST DO THE THINGS YOU THINK YOU CANNOT DO. - ELEANOR ROOSEVELT

184.

THE MORE DIFFICULT THE VICTORY, THE GREATER THE HAPPINESS IN WINNING. - PELE

185.

LIGHT TRAVELS FASTER THAN SOUND. THIS IS WHY SOME PEOPLE APPEAR BRIGHT UNTIL YOU HEAR THEM SPEAK. - ALAN DUNDES

186.

WHAT MATTERS MOST IN LIFE IS OFTEN INVISIBLE. - DUANE ELGIN

187.

I DON'T CARE THAT THEY STOLE MY IDEA. I CARE THAT THEY DON'T HAVE ANY OF THEIR OWN. - NIKOLA TESLA

188.

THE BAD NEWS IS TIME FLIES. THE GOOD NEWS IS YOU'RE THE PILOT. - MICHAEL ALTSHULER

189.

SPORTS ARE THE REASON I AM OUT OF SHAPE. I WATCH THEM ALL ON TV. - THOMAS SOWELL

190.

EVERYTHING YOU'VE EVER WANTED IS ON THE OTHER SIDE

OF FEAR. - GEORGE ADDAIR

191.

ALL PROGRESS TAKES PLACE OUTSIDE THE COMFORT ZONE.

- MICHAEL JOHN BOBAK

192.

ONLY THOSE WHO WILL RISK GOING TOO FAR CAN POSSIBLY

FIND OUT HOW FAR ONE CAN GO. - T. S. ELIOT

193.

TO LIVE IS THE RAREST THING IN THE WORLD. MOST PEOPLE

EXIST, THAT IS ALL. - OSCAR WILDE

194.

GOOD FRIENDS, GOOD BOOKS, AND A SLEEPY CONSCIENCE,

THIS IS THE IDEAL LIFE. - MARK TWAIN

195.

I AM NOT A PRODUCT OF MY CIRCUMSTANCES. I AM A PRODUCT OF MY DECISIONS. - STEPHEN COVEY

196.

THE SUCCESSFUL WARRIOR IS THE AVERAGE MAN, WITH LASER-LIKE FOCUS. - BRUCE LEE

197.

REAL EDUCATION STARTS WHEN YOU REALIZE THAT LIFE IS WILD AND YOU KNOW NOTHING ABOUT IT. - MAXIME LAGACE

198.

LIFE IS A MOUNTAIN. YOUR GOAL IS TO FIND YOUR PATH, NOT TO REACH THE TOP. - MAXIME LAGACE

199.

YOU'VE GOT TO GET UP EVERY MORNING WITH DETERMINATION IF YOU'RE GOING TO GO TO BED WITH SATISFACTION. - GEORGE LORIMER

200.

CARE ABOUT WHAT OTHER PEOPLE THINK AND YOU WILL ALWAYS BE THEIR PRISONER. - LAO TZU

201.

I ATTRIBUTE MY SUCCESS TO THIS. I NEVER GAVE OR TOOK ANY EXCUSE. - FLORENCE NIGHTINGALE

202.

TRY NOT TO BECOME A MAN OF SUCCESS BUT RATHER TO BECOME A MAN OF VALUE. - ALBERT EINSTEIN

203.

SOMETIMES THE QUESTIONS ARE COMPLICATED AND THE ANSWERS ARE SIMPLE. - DR. SEUSS

204.

CONFIDENCE IS 10 PERCENT WORK AND 90 PERCENT DELUSION. - TINA FEY

205.

NOBODY CAN PREDICT THE FUTURE. THE IDEA IS TO HAVE A FIRM GRASP OF THE PRESENT. - PETER F. DRUCKER

206.

DOING IS A QUANTUM LEAP FROM IMAGINING. - BARBARA SHER

207.

YOU ONLY LIVE ONCE, BUT IF YOU DO IT RIGHT, ONCE IS ENOUGH. - MAE WEST

208.

THINGS WORK OUT BEST FOR THOSE WHO MAKE THE BEST OF HOW THINGS WORK OUT. - JOHN WOODEN

209.

THE MORE YOU KNOW WHO YOU ARE, AND WHAT YOU WANT, THE LESS YOU LET THINGS UPSET YOU. - STEPHANIE PERKINS

210.

THE FUTURE BELONGS TO THOSE WHO BELIEVE IN THE BEAUTY OF THEIR DREAMS. - ELEANOR ROOSEVELT

211.

THE GUY WHO INVENTED THE FIRST WHEEL WAS AN IDIOT. THE GUY WHO INVENTED THE OTHER THREE WAS A GENIUS. - SID CAESAR

212.

LIFE SHRINKS OR EXPANDS IN PROPORTION TO ONE'S COURAGE. - ANAS NIN

213.

DO YOU THINK IT IS BETTER TO FAIL AT SOMETHING WORTHWHILE, OR SUCCEED AT SOMETHING MEANINGLESS. - TOMMY WALLACH

214.

ASK NOT WHAT YOUR COUNTRY CAN DO FOR YOU, BUT WHAT YOU CAN DO FOR YOUR COUNTRY. - JOHN F. KENNEDY

215.

IT ISN'T WHERE YOU CAME FROM. IT'S WHERE YOU'RE GOING

THAT COUNTS. - ELLA FITZGERALD

216.

LOOK DEEP INTO NATURE, AND THEN YOU WILL UNDERSTAND

EVERYTHING BETTER. - ALBERT EINSTEIN

217.

IF EVOLUTION REALLY WORKS, HOW COME MOTHERS ONLY

HAVE TWO HANDS? - MILTON BERLE

218.

MONEY IS NOT THE MOST IMPORTANT THING IN THE WORLD.

LOVE IS. FORTUNATELY, I LOVE MONEY. - JACKIE MASON

219.

WHETHER YOU THINK YOU CAN, OR YOU CAN'T, EITHER WAY

YOU'RE RIGHT. - HENRY FORD

220.

THE STARTING POINT OF ALL ACHIEVEMENT IS DESIRE. -
NAPOLEON HILL

221.

WE GENERATE FEARS WHILE WE SIT. WE OVERCOME THEM
BY ACTION. - DR. HENRY LINK

222.

IF YOU ARE NOT WILLING TO RISK THE USUAL, YOU WILL HAVE
TO SETTLE FOR THE ORDINARY. - JIM ROHN

223.

WE MAKE A LIVING BY WHAT WE GET, BUT WE MAKE A LIFE BY
WHAT WE GIVE. - WINSTON CHURCHILL

224.

IF YOU CAN DREAM IT, YOU CAN DO IT. - WALT DISNEY

225.

BE WILLING TO SACRIFICE WHAT YOU THINK YOU HAVE
TODAY FOR THE LIFE THAT YOU WANT TOMORROW. - NEIL
STRAUSS

226.

REMEMBER THAT NOT GETTING WHAT YOU WANT IS
SOMETIMES A WONDERFUL STROKE OF LUCK. - DALAI LAMA

227.

I'M THE ONE THAT'S GOT TO DIE WHEN IT'S TIME FOR ME TO
DIE, SO LET ME LIVE MY LIFE THE WAY I WANT TO. - JIMI
HENDRIX

228.

IT'S HARD TO BEAT A PERSON WHO NEVER GIVES UP. - BABE
RUTH

229.

EVERY MAN IS BORN AS MANY MEN AND DIES AS A SINGLE
ONE. - MARTIN HEIDEGGER

230.

FIND A VICTORY IN EVERY DEFEAT TO REMAIN HOPEFUL, AND FIND A DEFEAT IN EVERY VICTORY TO REMAIN HUMBLE. - ORRIN WOODWARD

231.

IF YOU WANT SOMETHING YOU'VE NEVER HAD, YOU MUST BE WILLING TO DO SOMETHING YOU'VE NEVER DONE. - THOMAS JEFFERSON

232.

EDUCATION COSTS MONEY. BUT THEN SO DOES IGNORANCE. - SIR CLAUS MOSER

233.

LIFE IS SO SHORT. I WOULD RATHER SING ONE SONG THAN INTERPRET THE THOUSAND. - JACK LONDON

234.

THE ROAD TO SUCCESS AND THE ROAD TO FAILURE ARE ALMOST EXACTLY THE SAME. - COLIN R. DAVIS

235.

TROUBLE KNOCKED AT THE DOOR, BUT, HEARING LAUGHTER, HURRIED AWAY. - BENJAMIN FRANKLIN

236.

THE ONLY WAY OF FINDING THE LIMITS OF THE POSSIBLE IS BY GOING BEYOND THEM INTO THE IMPOSSIBLE. - ARTHUR C. CLARKE

237.

LIFE ISN'T ABOUT FINDING YOURSELF. LIFE IS ABOUT CREATING YOURSELF. - GEORGE BERNARD SHAW

238.

ACT AS IF WHAT YOU DO MAKES A DIFFERENCE. IT DOES. - WILLIAM JAMES

239.

EVERY STRIKE BRINGS ME CLOSER TO THE NEXT HOME RUN. - BABE RUTH

240.

DON'T TAKE LIFE TOO SERIOUSLY. YOU'LL NEVER GET OUT OF IT ALIVE. - ELBERT HUBBARD

241.

THE DISTANCE BETWEEN INSANITY AND GENIUS IS MEASURED ONLY BY SUCCESS. - BRUCE FEIRSTEIN

242.

ENTHUSIASM MOVES THE WORLD. - ARTHUR BALFOUR

243.

DON'T DOWNGRADE YOUR DREAM JUST TO FIT YOUR REALITY. UPGRADE YOUR CONVICTION TO MATCH YOUR DESTINY. - STUART SCOTT

244.

BELIEVE YOU CAN AND YOU'RE HALFWAY THERE. - THEODORE ROOSEVELT

245.

THE LONGER I GO ABOUT LIVING, I SEE IT'S THE RELATIONSHIP THAT IS MOST MEANINGFUL. - WILLIAM SHATNER

246.

THE MOST IMPORTANT THINGS ARE THE HARDEST TO SAY, BECAUSE WORDS DIMINISH THEM. - STEPHEN KING

247.

YOUR PAIN IS THE BREAKING OF THE SHELL THAT ENCLOSES YOUR UNDERSTANDING. - KAHLIL GIBRAN

248.

YOUR PRESENT CIRCUMSTANCES DON'T DETERMINE WHERE YOU CAN GO. THEY MERELY DETERMINE WHERE YOU START. - NIDO QUBEIN

249.

SUCCESS IS HOW HIGH YOU BOUNCE WHEN YOU HIT BOTTOM. - GEORGE S. PATTON

250.

IT IS NEVER TOO LATE TO BE WHAT YOU MIGHT HAVE BEEN. - GEORGE ELIOT

251.

SOME MEN SEE THINGS AS THEY ARE AND SAY WHY? I DREAM THINGS THAT NEVER WERE AND SAY WHY NOT. - GEORGE BERNARD SHAW

252.

ALWAYS REMEMBER THAT YOU ARE ABSOLUTELY UNIQUE, JUST LIKE EVERYONE ELSE. - MARGARET MEAD

253.

MY DOCTOR GAVE ME SIX MONTHS TO LIVE, BUT WHEN I COULDN'T PAY THE BILL HE GAVE ME SIX MONTHS MORE. - WALTER MATHAU

254.

YOU ARE NEVER TOO OLD TO SET ANOTHER GOAL OR TO DREAM A NEW DREAM. - C.S. LEWIS

255.

PEOPLE DO NOT LACK STRENGTH, THEY LACK WILL. - VICTOR HUGO

256.

LOVE CONQUERS ALL THINGS EXCEPT POVERTY AND TOOTHACHE. - MAE WEST

257.

LIGHT TOMORROW WITH TODAY. - ELIZABETH BARRETT BROWNING

258.

IT DOES NOT MATTER HOW SLOWLY YOU GO SO LONG AS YOU DO NOT STOP. - CONFUCIUS

259.

A MAN WHO STANDS FOR NOTHING WILL FALL FOR ANYTHING. - MALCOLM X

260.

YOU DON'T ALWAYS NEED A PLAN. SOMETIMES YOU JUST

NEED TO BREATHE, TRUST, LET GO AND SEE WHAT HAPPENS.

- MANDY HALE

261.

LET YOUR ACTION MANIFEST YOUR THOUGHT, YOUR BELIEF

AND YOUR PASSION. - MOHAMMED ALI BAPIR

262.

NOTHING WILL WORK UNLESS YOU DO. - MAYA ANGELOU

263.

IF YOU DON'T LIKE SOMETHING CHANGE IT. IF YOU CAN'T

CHANGE IT, CHANGE THE WAY YOU THINK ABOUT IT. - MARY

ENGELBREIT

264.

NO ONE CAN COMPETE WITH YOU ON BEING YOU. MOST OF

LIFE IS A SEARCH FOR WHO AND WHAT NEEDS YOU THE

MOST. - NAVAL RAVIKANT

265.

WINNERS NEVER QUIT, AND QUITTERS NEVER WIN. - VINCE LOMBARDI

266.

EVERY NOW AND THEN IT'S GOOD TO STOP CLIMBING AND APPRECIATE THE VIEW FROM RIGHT WHERE YOU ARE. - LORI DESCHENE

267.

WHEN A MAN OPENS A CAR DOOR FOR HIS WIFE, IT'S EITHER A NEW CAR OR A NEW WIFE. - PRINCE PHILIP

268.

DO NOT GO WHERE THE PATH MAY LEAD, GO INSTEAD WHERE THERE IS NO PATH AND LEAVE A TRAIL. - RALPH WALDO EMERSON

269.

EVER TRIED. EVER FAILED. NO MATTER. TRY AGAIN. FAIL AGAIN. FAIL BETTER. - SAMUEL BECKETT

270.

IT'S NOT WHETHER YOU GET KNOCKED DOWN, IT'S WHETHER YOU GET UP. - VINCE LOMBARDI

271.

DON'T GAIN THE WORLD AND LOSE YOUR SOUL, WISDOM IS BETTER THAN SILVER OR GOLD. - BOB MARLEY

272.

IF NOT US, WHO? IF NOT NOW, WHEN? - JOHN F. KENNEDY 208

273.

ZEAL WITHOUT KNOWLEDGE IS FIRE WITHOUT LIGHT. - THOMAS HUXLEY

274.

THE CHIEF DANGER IN LIFE IS THAT YOU MAY TAKE TOO MANY PRECAUTIONS. - ALFRED ADLER

275.

EXPERIENCE IS NOT WHAT HAPPENS TO YOU, IT'S WHAT YOU DO WITH WHAT HAPPENS TO YOU. - ALDOUS HUXLEY

276.

I HAD PLASTIC SURGERY LAST WEEK. I CUT UP MY CREDIT CARDS. - HENNY YOUNGMAN

277.

YOU YOURSELF, AS MUCH AS ANYBODY IN THE ENTIRE UNIVERSE, DESERVE YOUR LOVE AND AFFECTION. - BUDDHA

278.

SOMEONE IS SITTING IN THE SHADE TODAY BECAUSE SOMEONE PLANTED A TREE A LONG TIME AGO. - WARREN BUFFETT

279.

IF LIFE IS A VIDEO GAME, THE GRAPHICS ARE GREAT, BUT THE PLOT IS CONFUSING AND THE TUTORIAL IS WAY TOO LONG. - ELON MUSK

280.

EITHER YOU RUN THE DAY, OR THE DAY RUNS YOU. - JIM
ROHN

281.

WHEN THINGS GO WRONG, DON'T GO WITH THEM. - ELVIS
PRESLEY

282.

THE FLAVOR OF LIFE IS ON THE EDGE. - NAVAL RAVIKANT

283.

YOUR MIND CAN BE EITHER YOUR PRISON OR YOUR PALACE.
WHAT YOU MAKE IT IS YOURS TO DECIDE - BERNARD KELVIN
CLIVE

284.

LIFE IS THE FLOWER FOR WHICH LOVE IS THE HONEY. -
VICTOR HUGO

285.

A BANK IS A PLACE THAT WILL LEND YOU MONEY IF YOU CAN PROVE THAT YOU DON'T NEED IT. - BOB HOPE

286.

DREAM AS IF YOU'LL LIVE FOREVER, LIVE AS IF YOU'LL DIE TODAY. - JAMES DEAN

287.

I ASKED GOD FOR A BIKE, BUT I KNOW GOD DOESN'T WORK THAT WAY. SO I STOLE A BIKE AND ASKED FOR FORGIVENESS. - EMO PHILIPS

288.

I TELL YOU, IN THIS WORLD BEING A LITTLE CRAZY HELPS TO KEEP YOU SANE. - ZSA ZSA GABOR

289.

I DON'T THINK OF ALL THE MISERY BUT OF THE BEAUTY THAT STILL REMAINS. - ANNE FRANK

290.

PEOPLE WHO ARE CRAZY ENOUGH TO THINK THEY CAN CHANGE THE WORLD, ARE THE ONES WHO DO. - ROB SILTANEN

291.

THOUGH NO ONE CAN GO BACK AND MAKE A BRAND NEW START, ANYONE CAN START FROM NOW AND MAKE A BRAND NEW ENDING. - CARL BARD

292.

ALL RIGHT EVERYONE, LINE UP ALPHABETICALLY ACCORDING TO YOUR HEIGHT. - CASEY STENGEL

293.

ONLY I CAN CHANGE MY LIFE. NO ONE CAN DO IT FOR ME. - CAROL BURNETT

294.

LIFE IS NOT ABOUT FINDING YOURSELF. LIFE IS ABOUT CREATING YOURSELF. - LOLLY DASKAL

295.

PUT YOUR HEART, MIND, AND SOUL INTO EVEN YOUR SMALLEST ACTS. THIS IS THE SECRET OF SUCCESS. - SWAMI SIVANANDA

296.

THE REAL OPPORTUNITY FOR SUCCESS LIES WITHIN THE PERSON AND NOT IN THE JOB. - ZIG ZIGLAR

297.

START WHERE YOU ARE. USE WHAT YOU HAVE. DO WHAT YOU CAN. - ARTHUR ASHE

298.

THE FUTURE BELONGS TO THOSE WHO PREPARE FOR IT TODAY. - MALCOLM X

299.

BE NOT AFRAID OF LIFE. BELIEVE THAT LIFE IS WORTH LIVING, AND YOUR BELIEF WILL HELP CREATE THE FACT. - WILLIAM JAMES

300.

LIFE'S TOO MYSTERIOUS TO TAKE TOO SERIOUS. - MARY
ENGELBREIT

301.

WHAT WE ACHIEVE INWARDLY WILL CHANGE OUTER
REALITY. - PLUTARCH

302.

LIFE IS LIKE RIDING A BICYCLE. TO KEEP YOUR BALANCE, YOU
MUST KEEP MOVING. - ALBERT EINSTEIN

303.

WE MUST BE WILLING TO LET GO OF THE LIFE WE PLANNED
SO AS TO HAVE THE LIFE THAT IS WAITING FOR US. - JOSEPH
CAMPBELL

304.

THE THOUGHTFUL SOUL TO SOLITUDE RETIRES. - OMAR
KHAYYAM

305.

MY LIFE IS MY MESSAGE. - MAHATMA GANDHI

306.

THE BEST THING ABOUT THE FUTURE IS THAT IT COMES ONE DAY AT A TIME. - ABRAHAM LINCOLN

307.

IF YOU WANT TO LIFT YOURSELF UP, LIFT UP SOMEONE ELSE. - BOOKER T. WASHINGTON

308.

THIS IS YOUR LIFE AND IT'S ENDING ONE MINUTE AT A TIME. - TYLER DURDEN

309.

AS A CHILD MY FAMILY'S MENU CONSISTED OF TWO CHOICES, TAKE IT OR LEAVE IT. - BUDDY HACKETT

310.

MEMORIES OF OUR LIVES, OF OUR WORKS AND OUR DEEDS WILL CONTINUE IN OTHERS. - ROSA PARKS

311.

EDUCATION IS LEARNING WHAT YOU DIDN'T EVEN KNOW YOU DIDN'T KNOW. - DANIEL J. BOORSTIN

312.

A DAY WITHOUT LAUGHTER IS A DAY WASTED. - CHARLIE CHAPLIN

313.

KEEP SMILING, BECAUSE LIFE IS A BEAUTIFUL THING AND THERE'S SO MUCH TO SMILE ABOUT. - MARILYN MONROE

314.

IF YOU REALLY LOOK CLOSELY, MOST OVERNIGHT SUCCESSES TOOK A LONG TIME. - STEVE JOBS

315.

ALL LIFE IS AN EXPERIMENT. THE MORE EXPERIMENTS YOU MAKE THE BETTER. - RALPH WALDO EMERSON

316.

YOUR FOCUS DETERMINES YOUR REALITY. - GEORGE LUCAS

317.

YOU MAY ONLY SUCCEED IF YOU DESIRE SUCCEEDING. YOU MAY ONLY FAIL IF YOU DO NOT MIND FAILING. - PHILIPPOS

318.

THE LONELY BECOME EITHER THOUGHTFUL OR EMPTY. - MASON COOLEY

319.

ACTION MAY NOT ALWAYS BRING HAPPINESS BUT THERE IS NO HAPPINESS WITHOUT ACTION. - BENJAMIN DISRAELI

320.

A SUCCESSFUL MAN IS ONE WHO CAN LAY A FIRM FOUNDATION WITH THE BRICKS OTHERS HAVE THROWN AT HIM. - DAVID BRINKLEY

321.

OUR PRIME PURPOSE IN THIS LIFE IS TO HELP OTHERS. AND IF YOU CAN'T HELP THEM, AT LEAST DON'T HURT THEM. - DALAI LAMA

322.

IF YOU FIND IT HARD TO LAUGH AT YOURSELF, I WOULD BE HAPPY TO DO IT FOR YOU. - GROUCHO MARX

323.

THE TRAGEDY IN LIFE DOESN'T LIE IN NOT REACHING YOUR GOAL. THE TRAGEDY LIES IN HAVING NO GOAL TO REACH. - BENJAMIN MAYS

324.

LIFE IS TOO IMPORTANT TO BE TAKEN SERIOUSLY. - OSCAR WILDE

325.

THE DIFFERENCE BETWEEN STUPIDITY AND GENIUS IS THAT GENIUS HAS ITS LIMITS. - ALBERT EINSTEIN

326.

THE QUIETER YOU BECOME, THE MORE YOU ARE ABLE TO HEAR. - RUMI

327.

SOMETIMES YOU WILL NEVER KNOW THE VALUE OF A MOMENT, UNTIL IT BECOMES A MEMORY. - DR. SEUSS

328.

IF YOU THINK NOBODY CARES IF YOU'RE ALIVE, TRY MISSING A COUPLE OF CAR PAYMENTS. - EARL WILSON

329.

A DIAMOND IS MERELY A LUMP OF COAL THAT DID WELL UNDER PRESSURE. - UNKNOWN

330.

YOU HAVE TO SEE FAILURE AS THE BEGINNING AND THE MIDDLE, BUT NEVER ENTERTAIN IT AS AN END. - JESSICA HERRIN

331.

TALKING ABOUT MUSIC IS LIKE DANCING ABOUT ARCHITECTURE. - STEVE MARTIN

332.

NOT HOW LONG, BUT HOW WELL YOU HAVE LIVED IS THE MAIN THING. - SENECA

333.

DON'T SPEND TIME BEATING ON A WALL, HOPING TO TRANSFORM IT INTO A DOOR. - COCO CHANEL

334.

CHANGE IS THE LAW OF LIFE. THOSE WHO LOOK ONLY TO THE PAST OR PRESENT ARE CERTAIN TO MISS THE FUTURE. - JOHN F. KENNEDY

335.

MAN NEVER MADE ANY MATERIAL AS RESILIENT AS THE HUMAN SPIRIT. - BERN WILLIAMS

336.

SOMETIMES YOU WIN, SOMETIMES YOU LEARN. - JOHN C. MAXWELL

337.

KNOWING WHAT MUST BE DONE DOES AWAY WITH FEAR. - ROSA PARKS

338.

IT'S TRUE HARD WORK NEVER KILLED ANYBODY, BUT I FIGURE, WHY TAKE THE CHANCE? - RONALD REAGAN

339.

LIVE LIFE TO THE FULLEST, AND FOCUS ON THE POSITIVE. - MATT CAMERON

340.

YOU DON'T HAVE TO SEE THE WHOLE STAIRCASE, JUST TAKE THE FIRST STEP. - MARTIN LUTHER KING JR

341.

YOU GET WHAT YOU GIVE. - JENNIFER LOPEZ

342.

LIFE IS NOT A PROBLEM TO BE SOLVED, BUT A REALITY TO BE EXPERIENCED. - SOREN KIERKEGAARD

343.

MOST PEOPLE OVERESTIMATE WHAT THEY CAN DO IN ONE YEAR AND UNDERESTIMATE WHAT THEY CAN DO IN TEN YEARS. - BILL GATES

344.

KEEP YOUR FACE TO THE SUNSHINE AND YOU CANNOT SEE A SHADOW. - HELEN KELLER

345.

BE ALONE, THAT IS THE SECRET OF INVENTION. BE ALONE, THAT IS WHEN IDEAS ARE BORN. - NIKOLA TESLA

346.

DO NOT LET WHAT YOU CANNOT DO INTERFERE WITH WHAT YOU CAN DO. - JOHN WOODEN

347.

IN A GENTLE WAY, YOU CAN SHAKE THE WORLD. - MAHATMA GANDHI

348.

LIFE IS A QUESTION AND HOW WE LIVE IT IS OUR ANSWER. - GARY KELLER

349.

LIGHTEN UP, JUST ENJOY LIFE, SMILE MORE, LAUGH MORE, AND DON'T GET SO WORKED UP ABOUT THINGS. - KENNETH BRANAGH

350.

THE AVERAGE DOG IS A NICER PERSON THAN THE AVERAGE PERSON. - ANDY ROONEY

351.

LIFE IS TOO DEEP FOR WORDS, SO DON'T TRY TO DESCRIBE IT, JUST LIVE IT. - C. S. LEWIS

352.

LIFE IS HARD. AFTER ALL, IT KILLS YOU. - KATHARINE HEPBURN

353.

I WOULD RATHER DIE OF PASSION THAN OF BOREDOM. - VINCENT VAN GOGH

354.

DIFFICULT AND MEANINGFUL WILL ALWAYS BRING MORE SATISFACTION THAN EASY AND MEANINGLESS. - MAXIME LAGACE

355.

THERE ARE TWO WAYS OF SPREADING LIGHT. TO BE THE CANDLE, OR THE MIRROR THAT REFLECTS IT. - EDITH WHARTON

356.

THE ONLY DISABILITY IN LIFE IS A BAD ATTITUDE. - SCOTT HAMILTON

357.

BE HAPPY FOR THIS MOMENT. THIS MOMENT IS YOUR LIFE. - OMAR KHAYYAM

358.

I'M ALWAYS DOING THINGS I CAN'T DO. THAT'S HOW I GET TO DO THEM. - PABLO PICASSO

359.

BE SO GOOD THEY CAN'T IGNORE YOU. - STEVE MARTIN

360.

WHAT YOU GET BY ACHIEVING YOUR GOALS IS NOT AS IMPORTANT AS WHAT YOU BECOME BY ACHIEVING YOUR GOALS. - ZIG ZIGLAR

361.

EVERY NOBLE WORK IS AT FIRST IMPOSSIBLE. - THOMAS CARLYLE

362.

STAY CLOSE TO ANYTHING THAT MAKES YOU GLAD YOU ARE ALIVE. - HAFEZ

363.

IN THE END, IT'S NOT THE YEARS IN YOUR LIFE THAT COUNT. IT'S THE LIFE IN YOUR YEARS. - ABRAHAM LINCOLN

364.

NEVER DO TOMORROW WHAT YOU CAN DO TODAY. PROCRASTINATION IS THE THIEF OF TIME. - CHARLES DICKENS

365.

IF YOU'RE OFFERED A SEAT ON A ROCKET SHIP, DON'T ASK WHAT SEAT, JUST GET ON. - SHERYL SANDBERG

366.

YOU HAVE BRAINS IN YOUR HEAD. YOU HAVE FEET IN YOUR SHOES. YOU CAN STEER YOURSELF ANY DIRECTION YOU CHOOSE. - DR. SEUSS

367.

WHATEVER THE MIND OF MAN CAN CONCEIVE AND BELIEVE, IT CAN ACHIEVE. - NAPOLEON HILL

368.

THE ONLY IMPOSSIBLE JOURNEY IS THE ONE YOU NEVER BEGIN. - TONY ROBBINS

369.

THE MORE UNINTELLIGENT A MAN IS, THE LESS MYSTERIOUS EXISTENCE SEEMS TO HIM. - ARTHUR SCHOPENHAUER

370.

WELL DONE IS BETTER THAN WELL SAID. - BENJAMIN FRANKLIN

371.

THE GREATEST GLORY IN LIVING LIES NOT IN NEVER FALLING, BUT IN RISING EVERY TIME WE FALL. - NELSON MANDELA

372.

IF LIFE WERE PREDICTABLE IT WOULD CEASE TO BE LIFE, AND BE WITHOUT FLAVOR. - ELEANOR ROOSEVELT

373.

OUR LIVES BEGIN TO END THE DAY WE BECOME SILENT ABOUT THINGS THAT MATTER. - MARTIN LUTHER KING JR.

374.

TODAY'S ACCOMPLISHMENTS WERE YESTERDAY'S IMPOSSIBILITIES. - ROBERT H. SCHULLER

375.

LIFE ISN'T A MATTER OF MILESTONES, BUT OF MOMENTS. - ROSE KENNEDY

376.

THERE IS MORE TO LIFE THAN INCREASING ITS SPEED. - MAHATMA GANDHI

377.

ONCE YOU'VE ACCEPTED YOUR FLAWS, NO ONE CAN USE THEM AGAINST YOU. - GEORGE R.R. MARTIN

378.

TOO OFTEN WE ENJOY THE COMFORT OF OPINION WITHOUT THE DISCOMFORT OF THOUGHT. - JOHN F. KENNEDY

379.

THE BEST WAY TO TEACH YOUR KIDS ABOUT TAXES IS BY EATING 30 PERCENT OF THEIR ICE CREAM. - BILL MURRAY

380.

ONLY A LIFE LIVED FOR OTHERS IS A LIFE WORTHWHILE. - ALBERT EINSTEIN

381.

TRY TO BE A RAINBOW IN SOMEONE ELSE'S CLOUD. - MAYA ANGELOU

382.

PERFECTION IS BORING. GETTING BETTER IS WHERE ALL THE FUN IS. - DRAGOS ROUA

383.

IF YOU GENUINELY WANT SOMETHING, DON'T WAIT FOR IT. TEACH YOURSELF TO BE IMPATIENT. - GURBAKSH CHAHAL

384.

BETTER A CRUEL TRUTH THAN A COMFORTABLE DELUSION. - EDWARD ABBEY

385.

DO WHAT YOU HAVE TO DO UNTIL YOU CAN DO WHAT YOU WANT TO DO. - OPRAH WINFREY

386.

PATIENCE WITH SMALL DETAILS MAKES PERFECT A LARGE WORK, LIKE THE UNIVERSE. - RUMI

387.

EVERYTHING IS FUNNY, AS LONG AS IT'S HAPPENING TO SOMEBODY ELSE. - WILL ROGERS

388.

NOWADAYS PEOPLE KNOW THE PRICE OF EVERYTHING AND THE VALUE OF NOTHING. - OSCAR WILDE

389.

EACH PERSON MUST LIVE THEIR LIFE AS A MODEL FOR OTHERS. - ROSA PARKS

390.

EIGHTY PERCENT OF SUCCESS IS SHOWING UP. - WOODY ALLEN

391.

LIFE IS A SUCCESSION OF LESSONS WHICH MUST BE LIVED TO BE UNDERSTOOD. - RALPH WALDO EMERSON

392.

THE TRUTH IS, EVERYONE IS GOING TO HURT YOU. YOU JUST GOT TO FIND THE ONES WORTH SUFFERING FOR. - BOB MARLEY

393.

ONE WAY TO KEEP MOMENTUM GOING IS TO HAVE CONSTANTLY GREATER GOALS. - MICHAEL KORDA

394.

IF YOU SPEND TOO MUCH TIME THINKING ABOUT A THING, YOU'LL NEVER GET IT DONE. - BRUCE LEE

395.

THE ONLY PLACE WHERE SUCCESS COMES BEFORE WORK IS IN THE DICTIONARY. - VIDAL SASSOON

396.

DON'T LIVE THE SAME YEAR 75 TIMES AND CALL IT A LIFE. - ROBIN SHARMA

397.

YOU ARE ENOUGH JUST AS YOU ARE. - MEGHAN MARKLE

398.

CHALLENGES, FAILURES, DEFEATS AND ULTIMATELY, PROGRESS, ARE WHAT MAKE YOUR LIFE WORTHWHILE. - MAXIME LAGACE

399.

LIFE IS MADE OF EVER SO MANY PARTINGS WELDED TOGETHER. - CHARLES DICKENS

400.

LIVE EACH DAY AS IF YOUR LIFE HAD JUST BEGUN. - JOHANN WOLFGANG VON GOETHE

401.

GET BUSY LIVING OR GET BUSY DYING. - STEPHEN KING

402.

BETTER TO REMAIN SILENT AND BE THOUGHT A FOOL THAN TO SPEAK OUT AND REMOVE ALL DOUBT. - ABRAHAM LINCOLN

403.

THE BEST WAY TO GET STARTED IS TO QUIT TALKING AND BEGIN DOING. - WALT DISNEY

404.

IN THE MIDDLE OF A DIFFICULTY LIES OPPORTUNITY. - ALBERT EINSTEIN

405.

LIFE IS SHORT, AND IT IS UP TO YOU TO MAKE IT SWEET. - SARAH LOUISE DELANY

406.

IT'S NOT THAT I'M SO SMART, IT'S JUST THAT I STAY WITH PROBLEMS LONGER. - ALBERT EINSTEIN

407.

IF YOU CAN IMAGINE IT, YOU CAN ACHIEVE IT. IF YOU CAN DREAM IT, YOU CAN BECOME IT. - WILLIAM ARTHUR WARD

408.

THE MIND IS EVERYTHING. WHAT YOU THINK YOU BECOME. - BUDDHA

409.

FAILURE IS THE CONDIMENT THAT GIVES SUCCESS IT'S FLAVOR. - TRUMAN CAPOTE

410.

LITTLE MINDS ARE TAMED AND SUBDUED BY MISFORTUNE BUT GREAT MINDS RISE ABOVE IT. - WASHINGTON IRVING

411.

CHANGE YOUR LIFE TODAY. DON'T GAMBLE ON THE FUTURE, ACT NOW, WITHOUT DELAY. - SIMONE DE BEAUVOIR

412.

BE KIND WHENEVER POSSIBLE. IT IS ALWAYS POSSIBLE. - DALAI LAMA

413.

THERE IS ONLY ONE WAY TO AVOID CRITICISM. DO NOTHING, SAY NOTHING, AND BE NOTHING. - ARISTOTLE

414.

EVERYONE THINKS OF CHANGING THE WORLD, BUT NO ONE THINKS OF CHANGING HIMSELF. - LEO TOLSTOY

415.

A BARGAIN IS SOMETHING YOU DON'T NEED AT A PRICE YOU CAN'T RESIST. - FRANKLIN JONES

416.

A FOOL THINKS HIMSELF TO BE WISE, BUT A WISE MAN KNOWS HIMSELF TO BE A FOOL. - WILLIAM SHAKESPEARE

417.

LIFE IS REALLY SIMPLE, BUT WE INSIST ON MAKING IT COMPLICATED. - CONFUCIUS

418.

OPPORTUNITIES DON'T HAPPEN, YOU CREATE THEM. - CHRIS GROSSER

419.

NEVER BEND YOUR HEAD. ALWAYS HOLD IT HIGH. LOOK THE WORLD STRAIGHT IN THE EYE. - HELEN KELLER

420.

WHOEVER SAID MONEY CAN'T BUY HAPPINESS DIDN'T KNOW WHERE TO SHOP. - GERTRUDE STEIN

421.

THE JOURNEY OF A THOUSAND MILES BEGINS WITH ONE STEP. - LAO TZU

422.

LIFE IS NOT A MATTER OF HOLDING GOOD CARDS, BUT OF PLAYING A POOR HAND WELL. - ROBERT LOUIS STEVENSON

423.

THE WEAK CAN NEVER FORGIVE. FORGIVENESS IS THE ATTRIBUTE OF THE STRONG. - MAHATMA GANDHI

424.

CERTAIN THINGS CATCH YOUR EYE, BUT PURSUE ONLY THOSE THAT CAPTURE THE HEART. - ANCIENT INDIAN PROVERB

425.

THE ONLY THING THAT INTERFERES WITH MY LEARNING IS MY EDUCATION. - ALBERT EINSTEIN

426.

THE BIGGEST ADVENTURE YOU CAN EVER TAKE IS TO LIVE THE LIFE OF YOUR DREAMS. - OPRAH WINFREY

427.

LIFE IS EITHER A DARING ADVENTURE OR NOTHING AT ALL. - HELEN KELLER

428.

NOBODY CAN GO BACK AND START A NEW BEGINNING, BUT ANYONE CAN START TODAY AND MAKE A NEW ENDING. - MARIA ROBINSON

429.

SUCCESS COMES FROM HAVING DREAMS THAT ARE BIGGER THAN YOUR FEARS. - BOBBY UNSER

430.

FOCUS ON THE JOURNEY, NOT THE DESTINATION. JOY IS FOUND NOT IN FINISHING AN ACTIVITY BUT IN DOING IT. - GREG ANDERSON

431.

GO CONFIDENTLY IN THE DIRECTION OF YOUR DREAMS. LIVE THE LIFE YOU'VE IMAGINED. - HENRY DAVID THOREAU

432.

IF I CANNOT DO GREAT THINGS, I CAN DO SMALL THINGS IN A GREAT WAY. - MARTIN LUTHER KING JR.

433.

IF YOU SURRENDER TO THE WIND, YOU CAN RIDE IT. - TONI MORRISON

434.

LIFE CHANGES VERY QUICKLY, IN A VERY POSITIVE WAY, IF YOU LET IT. - LINDSEY VONN

435.

WE BECOME WHAT WE THINK ABOUT MOST OF THE TIME, AND THAT'S THE STRANGEST SECRET. - EARL NIGHTINGALE

436.

YOU CAN COMPLAIN BECAUSE ROSES HAVE THORNS, OR YOU CAN REJOICE BECAUSE THORNS HAVE ROSES. - TOM WILSON

437.

IT'S NICE TO BE IMPORTANT, BUT IT'S ALSO IMPORTANT TO BE NICE. NEVER FORGET THAT. - SACHA BARON COHEN

438.

REMEMBER, TODAY IS THE TOMORROW YOU WORRIED ABOUT YESTERDAY. - DALE CARNEGIE

439.

ALWAYS GO TOO FAR, BECAUSE THAT'S WHERE YOU'LL FIND THE TRUTH. - ALBERT CAMUS

440.

WE AIM ABOVE THE MARK TO HIT THE MARK. - RALPH WALDO EMERSON

441.

I ALWAYS ARRIVE LATE AT THE OFFICE, BUT I MAKE UP FOR IT BY LEAVING EARLY. - CHARLES LAMB

442.

I USED TO JOG BUT THE ICE CUBES KEPT FALLING OUT OF MY GLASS. - DAVID LEE ROTH

443.

YOU CAN NEVER CROSS THE OCEAN UNTIL YOU HAVE THE COURAGE TO LOSE SIGHT OF THE SHORE. - CHRISTOPHER COLUMBUS

444.

IN THE END, IT'S NOT THE YEARS IN YOUR LIFE THAT COUNT. IT'S THE LIFE IN YOUR YEARS. - ABRAHAM LINCOLN

445.

DON'T WORRY ABOUT FAILURES, WORRY ABOUT THE CHANCES YOU MISS WHEN YOU DON'T EVEN TRY. - JACK CANFIELD

446.

BEHIND EVERY SUCCESSFUL MAN IS A SURPRISED MOTHER IN LAW. - VOLTAIRE

447.

THE TRICK IN LIFE IS LEARNING HOW TO DEAL WITH IT. - HELEN MIRREN

448.

EVERYONE HAS A PURPOSE IN LIFE. PERHAPS YOURS IS WATCHING TELEVISION. - DAVID LETTERMAN

449.

THE DIFFERENCE BETWEEN THE IMPOSSIBLE AND THE POSSIBLE LIES IN A PERSON'S DETERMINATION. - TOMMY LASORDA

450.

WE CAN'T HELP EVERYONE, BUT EVERYONE CAN HELP SOMEONE. - RONALD REAGAN

451.

IF SOMEONE ELSE IS PAYING FOR IT, FOOD JUST TASTES A LOT BETTER. - GILBERT GOTTFRIED

452.

I LIKE CRITICISM. IT MAKES YOU STRONG. - LEBRON JAMES

453.

EVERY SAINT HAS A PAST, AND EVERY SINNER HAS A FUTURE. - OSCAR WILDE

454.

KEEP YOUR FACE ALWAYS TOWARD THE SUNSHINE, AND SHADOWS WILL FALL BEHIND YOU. - WALT WHITMAN

455.

DO NOT WAIT TO STRIKE TILL THE IRON IS HOT BUT MAKE IT HOT BY STRIKING. - WILLIAM BUTLER YEATS

456.

YOU WILL FACE MANY DEFEATS IN LIFE, BUT NEVER LET YOURSELF BE DEFEATED. - MAYA ANGELOU

457.

NEVER PUT OFF TILL TOMORROW WHAT YOU CAN DO THE DAY AFTER TOMORROW. - MARK TWAIN

458.

LIFE IS WHAT HAPPENS WHEN YOU'RE BUSY MAKING OTHER PLANS. - JOHN LENNON

459.

IT ALWAYS SEEMS IMPOSSIBLE UNTIL IT'S DONE. - NELSON MANDELA

460.

LIFE IS A DARING ADVENTURE OR NOTHING AT ALL. - HELEN KELLER

461.

NOTHING IS COOLER AND MORE ATTRACTIVE THAN A BIG COMEBACK, AND THAT'LL BE ME. - STEVEN ADLER

462.

THE MERIT OF ALL THINGS LIES IN THEIR DIFFICULTY. - ALEXANDRE DUMAS

463.

IT IS NOT ENOUGH TO AIM, YOU MUST HIT. - ITALIAN PROVERB

464.

VERY LITTLE IS NEEDED TO MAKE A HAPPY LIFE. IT IS ALL WITHIN YOURSELF, IN YOUR WAY OF THINKING. - MARCUS AURELIUS

465.

KNOWLEDGE IS KNOWING A TOMATO IS A FRUIT. WISDOM IS NOT PUTTING IT IN A FRUIT SALAD. - MILES KINGTON

466.

LIFE IS PAIN. ANYONE WHO SAYS OTHERWISE IS SELLING SOMETHING. - WILLIAM GOLDMAN

467.

I NEVER DREAMED ABOUT SUCCESS, I WORKED FOR IT. - ESTEE LAUDER

468.

YOU MUST BE THE CHANGE YOU WISH TO SEE IN THE WORLD. - MAHATMA GANDHI

469.

IF YOU WANT TO LOOK THIN, HANG OUT WITH FAT PEOPLE. - RODNEY DANGERFIELD

470.

YOU CAN'T DEPEND ON YOUR EYES WHEN YOUR IMAGINATION IS OUT OF FOCUS. - MARK TWAIN

471.

THE DAY YOU STOP RACING, IS THE DAY YOU WIN THE RACE. - BOB MARLEY

472.

THE TEMPTATION OF THE AGE IS TO LOOK GOOD WITHOUT BEING GOOD. - BRENNAN MANNING

473.

YOUR BEST LIFE WILL NOT BE FOUND IN COMFORT. IT WILL BE FOUND IN FIGHTING FOR WHAT YOU BELIEVE IN. - MAXIME LAGACE

474.

BE MISERABLE. OR MOTIVATE YOURSELF. WHATEVER HAS TO BE DONE, IT'S ALWAYS YOUR CHOICE. - WAYNE DYER

475.

THERE ARE FAR, FAR BETTER THINGS AHEAD THAN ANY WE LEAVE BEHIND. - C.S. LEWIS

476.

BETTER TO DIE STANDING THAN TO LIVE ON YOUR KNEES. - ERNESTO

477.

THE SOUL WHICH HAS NO FIXED PURPOSE IN LIFE IS LOST. TO BE EVERYWHERE, IS TO BE NOWHERE. - MICHEL DE MONTAIGNE

478.

IF YOU WANT YOUR CHILDREN TO LISTEN, TRY TALKING SOFTLY TO SOMEONE ELSE. - ANN LANDERS

479.

TO ACCOMPLISH GREAT THINGS, WE MUST NOT ONLY ACT, BUT ALSO DREAM, NOT ONLY PLAN, BUT ALSO BELIEVE. - ANATOLE FRANCE

480.

NO MATTER WHAT YOU'RE GOING THROUGH, THERE'S A LIGHT AT THE END OF THE TUNNEL. - DEMI LOVATO

481.

IT IS NOT IN THE STARS TO HOLD OUR DESTINY BUT IN OURSELVES. - WILLIAM SHAKESPEARE

482.

INSPIRATION COMES FROM WITHIN YOURSELF. ONE HAS TO BE POSITIVE. WHEN YOU'RE POSITIVE, GOOD THINGS HAPPEN. - DEEP ROY

483.

I ALONE CANNOT CHANGE THE WORLD, BUT I CAN CAST A STONE ACROSS THE WATER TO CREATE MANY RIPPLES. - MOTHER TERESA

484.

YOU DON'T DROWN BY FALLING IN WATER. YOU DROWN BY STAYING THERE. - ROBERT COLLIER

485.

THE ONLY PERSON YOU SHOULD TRY TO BE BETTER THAN, IS THE PERSON YOU WERE YESTERDAY. - MATTY MULLENS

486.

WHAT SEEMS TO US AS BITTER TRIALS ARE OFTEN BLESSINGS IN DISGUISE. - OSCAR WILDE

487.

MAKE SURE YOUR WORST ENEMY DOESN'T LIVE BETWEEN YOUR OWN TWO EARS. - LAIRD HAMILTON

488.

EARLY TO BED AND EARLY TO RISE MAKES A MAN HEALTHY, WEALTHY, AND WISE. - BENJAMIN FRANKLIN

489.

YOU MISS 100 PERCENT OF THE SHOTS YOU NEVER TAKE. - WAYNE GRETZKY

490.

TELL ME AND I FORGET. TEACH ME AND I REMEMBER. INVOLVE ME AND I LEARN. - BENJAMIN FRANKLIN

491.

WE DO NOT REMEMBER DAYS, WE REMEMBER MOMENTS. - CESARE PAVESE

492.

LIFE ISN'T ABOUT FINDING YOURSELF. LIFE IS ABOUT CREATING YOURSELF. - GEORGE BERNARD SHAW

493.

EVEN THE FINEST SWORD PLUNGED INTO SALT WATER WILL

EVENTUALLY RUST. - SUN TZU

494.

HAPPINESS IS NOT BY CHANCE, BUT BY CHOICE. - JIM ROHN

495.

KEEP YOUR EYES ON THE STARS, AND YOUR FEET ON THE

GROUND. - THEODORE ROOSEVELT

496.

CHANGE YOUR THOUGHTS AND YOU CHANGE YOUR WORLD.

- NORMAN

497.

I FIND THAT THE HARDER I WORK, THE MORE LUCK I SEEM TO

HAVE. - THOMAS JEFFERSON

498.

A MAN SEES IN THE WORLD WHAT HE CARRIES IN HIS HEART.

- JOHANN WOLFGANG VON GOETHE

499.

MY FAVORITE MACHINE AT THE GYM IS THE VENDING

MACHINE. - CAROLINE RHEA

500.

WITHOUT ORDER NOTHING CAN EXIST, WITHOUT CHAOS

NOTHING CAN EVOLVE. – ANON

Free Book

100 Large Print

Sudoku Puzzles

Please go to the below URL to download your FREE Copy.

https://bit.ly/free-sudoku

Want More Books?

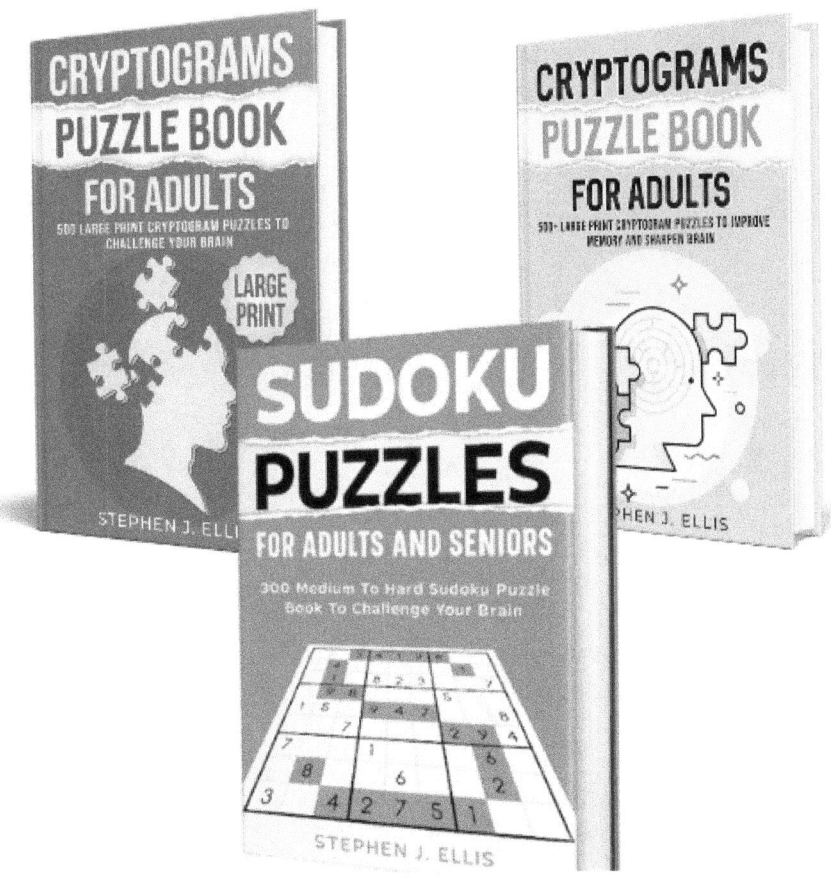

Please go to the below URL and check our other books.

https://bit.ly/stephenbooks